All you need to know about Buying and Selling your Property.

Every care is taken in the preparation of this book. The author and the publishers cannot accept responsibility for the consequences of any error in this book, however it may cause. This book is to be used for guidance purposes only for both Sellers and Buyers and no liability can be accepted for loss or expense incurred as a result of any statement that is made within this book.

First Edition 2011

Published by Paul Hardial

Printed by Lulu.com

Cover Illustrated by Helen Hardial

© Copyright: Paul Hardial 2011

ISBN: 978-1-4477-6958-3

Dedication

To my loving wife Maria and my daughter Helen, without whose help and support this book would not have been possible.

Acknowledgement

I would like to thank my sister, Annette and her husband Jack for their contribution to this book.

Preface

This book:-

- Provides a simple and effective step-by-step guide for anyone to use in the buying and selling of their property. It explains the transactions that take place in the process of buying and selling.

- Sets out the process of buying and selling a property in a language than you can understand. It takes you through the step-by-step process and also identifies the problem and gives you the solutions.

- Clearly explains the whole buying and selling process from choosing and arranging mortgages, the role of the solicitors, a variety of methods for buying and selling property, the preparation needed for both buyers and sellers to get the best deal, how to negotiate with confidence, the area and chain links property.

Most importantly I hope that the contents within this book give you a better understanding and the confidence to take the next step that will change your life for the better.

"Good Luck"

About the Author

The author has bought and renovated properties for many years. At present he works in the property industry as an adviser and as an investor.

He has been advising people buying and selling property throughout the U.K. He now owns his own Energy Company. Buying and selling is a complex and stressful business experience, no matter how many properties that you have brought or sold throughout the years, each one has it own story to tell as there are always new legal requirements and new things to consider.

The hope is that when you read this book it will take away all the uncertainty, complexity, provide you with a better understanding and knowledge experience to make the selling or buying process, smoother, and with a quick result to your satisfaction.

"When you are buying or selling a property you have to consider the present and future needs"

2. CONTENTS

1. INTRODUCTION

How to avoid the pitfalls that other buyers and sellers faced when buying or selling their property for the first time.

Buying or selling your property is one of the most important decisions that you are going to make in your life, no matter what others tell you about the process. The decision at the end of the day is one that only you can make. With the aid of this book, I am going to try and help by providing some facts and information that you will need to make your decision a lot easier.

It is estimated that 1.5 million people in England and Wales move homes each year. The system that we use today still involves a lot of money, time and stress. This is the case for those who are buying and selling.

The Government as at 21st May 2010 has suspended the Home Information Pack that was introduced by the previous Government. The seller now only has to produce and Energy Performance Certificate (EPC) within 28 days of marketing their property. This will be dealt in detail under the heading- 'Contents of Energy Performance Certificate'. The buyer is now responsible for all the Legal and Conveyancing process. When the new EPC Regulation comes into force, it will mean that an EPC will be required within 7 days of commencement of marketing for a property. Trading Standards Officers (TSO) will be given more powers to request and enforce the EPC from Vendors, Agents and Landlords. This new Regulation should have come into force on 1st July 2011. This has now been delayed until further notice by the Department for Communities and Local Government (DCLG).

This book illustrates the process of buying and selling your property, in most cases the process can be straightforward, if the correct decisions care, knowledge and having the right guidance are followed. By taking the correct professional advice and with the knowledge that you have gained from reading this book, the process of buying and selling should be a great deal easier. Throughout this book I have tried to provide a balance view and judgment for both buyers and sellers. I have also pinpointed what matters most without leaving out the basic points of buying and selling.

Due to a weak economic recovery, there is the possibility of a rise in unemployment, higher fuel prices, tighter control over lending by the banks and a requirement for larger deposits. There is also the possibility of higher interest rates to control inflation. Household incomes will be under pressure as the cost of living continues to rise with very little prospect of an increase in salaries. The value of property will continue to fall at least until the end of 2012. The more overvalued, the property market is, the sharper the falls in prices are likely to be. It is a great market to be in if you are a cash buyer as there are a wide range of property bargains.

The present economic conditions mean there will be a more stable property market throughout 2011, unlike the boom period of 2006, with sellers setting their prices of their property at a realistic level to sell their property quickly and avoid holding out for an unrealistic price. Agents and sellers who overvalued property will not sell as no buyer will consider a property which does not meet the present market conditions. The government estimates that there are currently over 1.4 million households who want to own their own property, but are unable to do so because property prices are unaffordable and the lack of mortgages that are available to buyers.

"Wishing you every success with a quick sale or purchase of your property"

2. BUYING A PROPERTY

Introduction

When considering the prospect of buying a home, it may be our first or second, the decisions are always the same to certain extent. That is, can we afford to buy, what is the area like, the neighbours, does the area have local facilities and amenities that we are used to, what about the school in the area and many more decisions that will be rushing through our mind when we think about buying our property. Buying your first home is one of the most exciting experiences of your life, but it is also a whole new world, and of course the expense involved in buying your home. The questions we keep asking ourselves are, where shall we move to, what is the area like, the cost of buying, the legal work, negotiations, dealing with surveyors and solicitors, finding a good mortgage deal and worrying about your deal falling through, on top of actually finding a home of your dreams. This involves a lot of work that can be very stressful at time, but can also be fun and exciting as well if you plan each step of the way. It can prove to be a surprisingly expensive business at a time when money is tight. Looking for a new home is a time-consuming process and it is tempting just to rush into buying the first one you like the look of. Once you have decided to buy a house and found out how much you can afford, it is worth sitting down and thinking hard about what you want from your new home and what your needs are. Local issues, such as schools, new developments and the future of big local employers affect prices.

Buying a property is going to be one of the biggest financial decisions that you will possible make in your life. It is not like going to buy a loaf of bread from the supermarket. Buying a property can be a lengthy and complicated business. It gives you unnecessary stress and worry. But luckily there is a lot of good advice around to help you to make your home buying experience as easy and problem free as possible. Hopefully by reading this book it will help, guide you and give you a better understanding of the home buying process. It is important to have a good understanding of the process involved as it will help you to avoid some of the most common hazards of home buying. Below is a reference guide to the steps that you need to follow and make your buying process a lot easier for you and also what to expect, how it all works, how to plan it and what to watch out for.

If you are only buying your own home as an investment in property you may find the next couple of years a little disappointing. Most predictions for house prices for 2011 are that they will be lower by the end of the year than the beginning. I do not see any sustained house price growth re-emerging until 2013. If you are buying properties to make money over the short term then do not buy at the moment. Now is a good time to buy property for a long term investment because of the fall in property prices over the last few years.

After finding a property you like, which can take anything from a few days to many months, the whole process from having your offer accepted to completion of the sale takes about 10 - 14 weeks. House buying in Britain is a slow process unlike many other countries.

Buying a property with Registered Title and Unregistered Title

There are two types of titles when buying a property in England and Wales: -

- Registered Title
- Unregistered Title

With Registered Title the documents prove that the seller owns the property and therefore has the right to sell it. These documents are available form the Land Registry who will provide you with an up to date Official Record of who owns the Land.

With regards to unregistered property, this is a bit more complex as it involves going through details of previous conveyances to ascertain as to who owns the property. If there are any disputes with the property you are going to buy as to the sellers title, my best advice is to walk away from the purchase and seek an alternative property that ownership has been proved, otherwise this will be a costly drawn out process. If you wish to proceed it can be a time consuming process so allow for this if you know that the property you are selling is an unregistered property. An official search of the index map can be obtained from the Land Registry and all the documents that the seller has to rely upon as evidence of title to the property that they have a right to sell. Either a solicitor or a professional person who knows how to create a title search creates an Epitome of Title. It is something like the BBC Television programmes about the Heir Hunters, tracing back the family tree line.

The cost of buying an unregistered property is significantly higher than that of a registered property. Once the seller can prove ownership then the title can be transferred to you, the new buyer of the property and be registered with the Land Registry.

How much can you afford?

Before looking at properties, you should consult a lender or mortgage adviser as to what your maximum possible loan would be. This will be based on the size of your deposit and how much you earn. All buyers need to put down a deposit on the property; a mortgage lender will rarely pay the whole price of the property. You should try to put down at least 5-10 per cent of the value of the home as a deposit, and more if possible. The smaller the deposit you put down, the more your lender will charge you for the extra risk. Most mortgage lenders charge a Mortgage Indemnity Guarantee fee (MIG), or a fee for loaning a higher percentage of the value, on bigger loans. If you do not have enough money for the deposit, for example if your house is not sold yet, it is possible to get a bridging loan from your bank, which will be repayable on the sale of your house.

Lenders in the past have provided mortgage loans based on a multiple of your salary. For example a lender will usually lend up to three times the size of your annual income, though some will lend up to four times your income. If you are buying as a couple, this increase to two-and-a-half times your joint income.

Recently it has become more common for Lenders to make an affordability assessment when calculating how much they are prepared to lend you. They will take into consideration your total disposable income together with all expenditures such as other loans, credit card, household bills and living expenses. The Lender will now consider how much you can afford to repay and how much they are prepared to lend you. Your lender may contact your employer to confirm your income, or if you are self-employed and taking out a self-certificate deal you may have to supply proof of your income.

The financial crisis that started in 2007 led to changes in mortgage lending. One of the consequences was a limit on the amount of finance banks and lenders have available, making them more cautious and less likely to take risks. Deals for those with small deposits, such as 100 per cent mortgages, were commonplace prior to 2007 but have become increasingly rare. The key to successfully gaining a mortgage approval is not only having a large deposit but also being a low risk level in the eyes of lenders. Check your credit score through credit referencing agencies. Make sure any missed payments you may have forgotten about are addressed. There are a number of different financial institutions which offer loans to people buying a property, for example, building societies, banks and loan brokers. You should find out if you are able to borrow money and if so, how much.

In the past this was an easy issue because lenders simply offered a multiple of your income, for instance two and a half times your salary. Now, because of the level of unsecured debt many of us carry, and the information available from credit agencies, most lenders use credit scoring and affordability techniques. If you have little debt then up to four times your salary might be available. As a first step, look at a lender's website and search out their affordability calculators and see how you fare. This simple task might remove all hope of buying at the moment, or confirm that you can make the sums work.

Some Building Societies now provide buyers with a certificate that states that a loan will be available provided the property is satisfactory. You may be able to get this certificate before you start looking for a property. Building Societies state that this certificate may help you to have your offer accepted by the seller, before finally deciding how much to spend on a property. You need to be sure you will have enough money to pay for all the additional costs. These include:-

- Survey fees.
- Valuation fees.
- Stamp Duty Land Tax.
- Land registry fee.
- Local authority searches.

- Fees, if any, charged by the mortgage lender or someone who arranges the mortgage, for example, a mortgage broker.
- The buyer solicitor's costs.
- VAT.
- Removal expenses.
- Any final bills, for example, gas and electricity, from your present home which will have to be paid when you move.
- Energy Performance Certificate.

You should be aware that if you start the process of buying a property and then the sale falls through you may have already paid for a valuation or a survey. If the solicitor has started any legal work you may also have to pay for the work done.

You should also take into account the running expenses of the property you wish to buy. These may include:-

- Council tax.
- Water rates.
- Ground rent, if the property is leasehold.
- Service charges, if the property is a leasehold flat.
- Insurance costs, including life insurance, buildings and contents insurance.
- Heating bills.

You will have to pay a deposit on exchange of contracts a few weeks before the purchase is completed and the money is received from the mortgage lender. The deposit is often 10% of the purchase price of the home but it can vary according to the lenders criteria.

Choosing a new area to live

The location

The immediate locality should also be an important part of your consideration as you view the property. When you are considering moving to a new area, there are a number of things, you may want to look at before making your decision, for example looking for a new job, or move to somewhere that has better schools or more green spaces.

By doing as much research as you possibly can on properties within your chosen area, it will make it less likely that you will waste your time seeing something that does not meet your needs or criteria. You can find out a lot about a new area to help you decide whether you want to move there or not. There are a lot of local information that are available on Government and local council's websites that may be of interest to you when you are looking for a home to buy:-

- Future planning developments
- Council tax bands and charges
- Local jobs and careers information
- School admission information
- Local parks and recreation areas
- Sports facilities
- Arts and leisure events and facilities
- Facilities for young people

You should also make sure the location meets your requirements, so here are a few things to think about when choosing somewhere to live:-

- How close is it to rail lines, motorways, or aircraft flight paths?

- What is the condition of nearby property like?
- Is the property near relevant transport links?
- What is the crime level like in the area?
- What are the neighbours like? Are they nice?
- The feel of the community - does it seem friendly?
- Does the property get enough natural light?
- Is the property well maintained?
- The age of the property?
- Garden size?
- What is the public transport like in the area?
- Are the local schools good?
- What are the local amenities like - shops, hospitals,
- What is the crime level like in the area?
- Jobs prospects?
- The environment?
- Schools and Childcare information?

How to find a property

Looking in estate agents windows, newspapers, the internet is also an excellent research tool for finding properties. There are now many websites specifically geared for property searches, as well as those catering for people who want to sell without an agent altogether. Most estate agents also have their own websites. There are a number of ways in which you could find a property to buy:-

- Using estate agents.
- Looking at the property pages in local newspapers.
- Contacting house building companies for details of new properties being built in the area.
- Looking on the internet.

Deciding on a property

When you find a property you should arrange to look at it to make sure it is what you will need and to get some idea of whether or not you will have to spend any additional money on the property, for example, for repairs or decoration. It is common for a potential buyer to visit a property two or three times before deciding to make an offer.

Types of Properties

Freehold property

If the property is freehold, this means that the land on which the property is built is part of the sale and no ground rent or service charge is payable.

Leasehold property

A property may be leasehold, which means that the land on which the property is built is not part of the sale. You have to pay ground rent to the owner of the land - who is called the freeholder.

The length of a lease can vary and you should check that the length of the lease on the property you are interested in buying is acceptable to the mortgage lender. In addition to ground rent on a leasehold property, you may have to pay an annual service charge. This usually happens with a flat. The service charge covers such items as maintenance and repairs to the buildings, cleaning of common parts and looking after the grounds.

A group of leaseholders living in the same building may have a right to jointly buy the freehold of the building or take over its management. In England and Wales, you can get further advice about leasehold from. The Leasehold Advisory Service.

Commonhold property

If the property is commonhold, this means that you can buy the freehold of the flat and own common parts of the building jointly with the owners of other flats in the building (known as a Commonhold Association).

In commonhold a ground rent or service charge is not payable. However, a share of the commonhold association's expenditure on maintenance, insurance and administration will be payable for the common parts of the building.

PROPERTY VIEWING

Do not waste your time and energy visiting properties that are outside your price range or unsuitable, only choose to go and view properties that are suitable, this way you can find your ideal home a lot faster and within your price range.

Take with you a pen and paper so that you can take notes of each property that you have visited noting the advantages and disadvantages of each property. When viewing properties try and be as comfortable as possible, that is with clothing and footwear so that you are not distracted or irritable when viewing a property.

Leave the children with friends or relatives, so that all your attention focused on the property you are viewing. Try to go with someone else. Your partner is best, but anyone whose opinion you trust is worth taking along - they may spot something you miss, or stop you getting carried away. View the properties as soon as possible. Leave it too long and you could lose out.

If you are tempted to buy a run-down property to renovate and sell on at a profit, check how long it has been on the market. If it has been there a long time, it suggests there is not a lot of profit to be made. Find out more in our renovating for profit section. New carpets, bathrooms and kitchens can be signs of a superficial renovation that is hiding more serious work to be done. Do not be afraid to visit your local tradesman to find out what the cost of the repair will be.

Viewing

Make a thorough set of notes for each property you view, especially if you are viewing a lot of properties in one go. It can be incredibly difficult to remember the little things, which may sway your opinion one way or another.

Do not let the agent rush you. It is irrelevant how busy they are. If this is going to be your new home, you should take your time and view the property at your own pace. Try to be friendly to the owner. If you do end up buying from them then a good relationship can make things a bit smoother. It may not make any difference at all to the sale, but it may make you feel good.

You should really have a thorough look at everything. Pay particular attention to anything that you have given top priority to.

Here is a list of things to check while you are in the property:-

- The general state of repairs. If the whole thing is basically sound, but in need of a facelift, make sure you are either going to be able to afford and make the alterations or can live with the state of the place until you can.

- The condition of the bathroom. Lots of limescale is a sign of hard water while discoloured patches can be an indication that the room is poorly ventilated.
- The kitchen units. Check that all the doors and drawers work properly.
- The condition of the Central Heating System.
- The windows. Are they double glazed?
- Check for damp and subsidence. Look out for cracks around the windows and doors. An uneven roofline, musty smells, brand new paint or wallpaper could be concealing something. Feel the walls for signs of moisture.
- Do you need a full survey or just the mortgage valuation survey?
- Try to get a view of the roofing. Look out for missing tiles. If it is raining, see if the drains and gutter appear to be working properly.
- Are there enough power points?
- Is there enough space? The way people set out their furniture can make it seem like there is more or less space than you will need.
- If you are thinking of buying, check out the state of some of the other houses on the street. If they do not look in the best state now, think what they might be like in a few years when you may be trying to sell.
- Take someone else with you if you can, preferably someone with different tastes who can spot things that you miss.
- Make sure you view the property during the day when you will be able to see better and spot problems
- If you really like a property, try to arrange to view it again at a different time of the day to give you a different perspective
- Try not to view too many properties in one day

- Take your time looking round the property
- Do not be afraid to ask direct and blunt questions about the property

If you believe the property has potential, arrange for a second viewing to see how it feels the second time around. You might want to take a friend whose opinion you value to come with you.

Given what a major transaction a house purchase is, buyers often spend a surprisingly tiny amount of time assessing the properties they are considering. Arm yourself with all the necessary information about the property and prepare a list of questions to ask. A checklist should help you prepare for property viewings to get the most out of your property search.

- Before you arrive for the viewing, do your homework on the property for sale and the local area so you avoid wasting any time on an unsuitable property.
- Here are a few things to bear in mind and questions you may want to ask once you are at the property.

Inside the property

Look out for the following when you are inside the property

- Is it a listed building or in a conservation area which might restrict any alterations?
- Is there central heating?
- Is there a loft?
- Are the windows double glazed?
- Has the property been altered in any way?
- Has the property been recently decorated?

- Is there enough storage for all your belongings?
- Does the property get enough natural light?
- Has it been well maintained?
- Could you see yourself living there?
- Does the property need updating - if so, how much will this cost?
- Are the rooms big enough for your needs - furniture, etc?
- What are the views like?
- How the water is heated - combination boiler or tank, etc?
- Is there any sign of subsidence, like major cracks in the walls or the doors sticking?
- Is there a smell of damp or any other sign such as the walls feeling damp, wallpaper peeling, paint bubbling, watermarks or mould?
- Do the window frames have cracking paint? If you can press your finger easily into the wood is it rotten?
- Are there enough power points - how old do they look?
- Does it feel like it could be your home?

Questions to ask the seller

Below are some of the questions that you can ask the sellers about the property. If this is going to be your future home it is important that you ask as many questions as possible and keep on asking until you are comfortable with the answers given to you. The more that you know about the property, the better equipped you are to make a sound judgment and decision on the property. When viewing a property it is easy to forget to ask important questions.

Here some more questions for you to ask the seller or the agent showing you round the property:-

- How many people have you had to view this property?
- What is the cost of Council Tax?
- Have you had any offers for this property so far?
- Is this property in a chain?
- Why are you selling?
- What is included in the sale?
- Do you want a quick sale?
- How long has the property been on the market?
- Will you accept a lower asking price for the sale?
- Has the property has ever been burgled while you have lived here?
- What comes with the property?
- If there is a loft, has this been insulated - if so, how long ago?
- Does the house have full central heating - if so, how old is it?
- Does the property have cavity wall insulation?
- Has the property been altered in any way - if so is the relevant planning and building control consents available to inspect?
- What are the neighbours like? Are they noisy?
- Has there ever been a dispute with the neighbours or anyone living nearby?
- What work have you had done on the property recently?
- How much are the utility bills generally?
- Have you an Energy Performance Certificate for the property?

CHAIN FREE PROPERTY

Buying a chain free property is often particularly beneficial to first time buyers, or those without an existing house to sell, who could find themselves the owners of a new home within just weeks of searching.

Most houses on the market are dependent on a sequence of other property sales and purchases. Chain free indicates a property with no such sequence.

Most houses on the market are part of a chain. This means the sale is dependent on a sequence of other property purchases and sales, as sellers will also be looking for a house to buy. Chain links houses that are being purchased where each is dependant on the sale of the next one in the chain; if one of these sales fall through then the whole chain of purchases can fail and affect numerous buyers and sellers as a result, usually the bigger the chain, the bigger the impact.

This can happen for a number of reasons, for example:-

- The seller may have already bought a new home and vacated the property.
- The seller is not buying a new home.
- The property is a new build.
- The property has been repossessed.

The benefits of buying chain free

The sale of a chain free property:-

- Is simpler and faster than in a chain.
- Has less risk of falling through.

A chain can add a great deal of time, expense and risk to the buying process, as there are far more people involved. All the properties in the chain are linked, and if one part of the chain fails it can impact on every stage. A break in the chain can therefore be heartbreaking because it can not only add to the expense of the selling and buying process but means delays are almost inevitable. A chain free property, however, can present much greater peace of mind for the purchaser.

Chain free properties are often new homes or vacant properties where the seller has already bought a new home or is not buying another property. Usually there is only one property, one buyer and one seller and so it's much easier in terms of dealing with valuations, survey reports and even legal titles.

Chain Link

Whenever you are involved in a move you are reliant on other people and their behaviour. Each person involved in a chain has the capacity to change their mind and there is the potential for problems to occur relating to particular links in the chain. A buyer or seller might lose their job or they might split from a partner and their buying situation might change. Or it could be technically related to the property in regards to problems revealed in a survey for example. Being chain free is a very big plus for a property. In the current market there is a lack of properties and high demand, many sellers are moving into rented accommodation, just so they can put themselves in a stronger position by removing the onward chain.

Chain free is a very good situation for buyers to be in. If you are in a chain, you are a risk to the vendor, whereas no chain equals confidence in their minds. In the end, the seller's decision will be what the position of the buyers in the chain is. No one wants the risk of holding up a chain or stopping the chain to progress down the link.

One in three property chains fall apart. This can happen for numerous reasons, from one party not having their finances in order, to an unpleasant surprise in the survey. The best way to ensure a chain progresses smoothly is through good communication. Stay in regular contact with your conveyancer and estate agent to make sure everything possible is being done to speed things along. It can also help to stay flexible. Be prepared to move in with your family or rent as a short-term measure if it means you can keep the chain going.

Buying chain free is often particularly beneficial to first time buyers, or those without an existing house to sell, who could find themselves the owners of a new home within just weeks of searching.

POTENTIAL COST OF BUYING YOUR HOME

When you have decided that you are buying a property, you should calculate exactly how much you can afford. On top of the cost of the house itself, there are many other, one-off expenses involved in buying a home and moving which can add up to figures from £2,000 to £6,000. In order to get a good idea of what sort of home you can realistically hope to buy, you also need to take these extra costs into account. To help you do your calculations, here is a guide to work out how much money you have to spend and what the costs will be. Do not forget you have to pay stamp duty land tax, as, with the recent inflation of property prices, for properties over £250,000 this has become a major consideration.

Calculating Your Price Range

You need to work out -

- The amount you will get from the sale of any current home.
- The amount you can borrow.
- The amount you have in savings or investments which you can use.
- Once you have done this, work out how much the other one-off costs of buying and moving will add up to.
- Deduct this from the above total calculation and you will have a rough estimate of the kind of price range you are looking at.

The One-Off Costs

Arrangement Fee

Arrangement fees for mortgages have risen over the past few years and as a result of the present UK financial markets, now costing several hundred pounds depending on the product you choose to buy. Some mortgage lenders will allow you to add the fee on to your total mortgage so you don't have to pay it upfront, though of course if you do this, you will be charged interest on the higher amount, while others may offer reduced fees in exchange for higher interest rates. A fee charged by lenders to cover the cost of setting up the mortgage. Some lenders may waive this fee.

Survey

When you are thinking about buying a property it is a good idea to find out whether there are any problems with the structure. You should also know if any repairs or alterations need to be made. A property survey may save you time and money in the long run if you uncover expensive defects before you buy. There are different types of survey to choose from according to the amount of information and advice you require about the property. When you are buying a home it is important to get a report about the property's overall condition. This can help uncover any work that may need to be done to the property before you buy.

Type of Survey

As a buyer there are three main types of survey to choose from:

A valuation

A valuation tells the lender how much the property is worth and will usually be carried out by your mortgage company if you need a mortgage to buy the property. The mortgage lender commissions this but you must cover the cost. The cost of the valuation depends on the value of the property, for example; allow about £135 for a property worth £50,000, £175 for a £100,000 house and so on. Some lenders do not charge this fee, as an incentive for you to take out a mortgage with them.

The valuation which is done for whoever is lending the money is not a survey. You should consider whether or not to have an independent survey carried out in addition to the valuation. The survey would not only consider the value of the property but would also examine the structure of the property and should identify any existing or potential problems.

A Homebuyer survey and valuation

The second is a homebuyer's report, which will cost around £400, depending on where you live. This valuable report will tell you about any problems with the property, such as whether it suffers from damp. While the cost may seem an unnecessary expense, it could end up saving you money, if any problems are found, you can renegotiate with the seller to cover the bills for putting them right. A homebuyer survey reports on defects in the property, its condition and value.

Building Survey

Third is the structural survey, which is often carried out on older or more unusual properties. The cost will depend on the size and type of the property, and can be around £1000, but it is worthwhile if you are buying something out of the ordinary. This type of survey provides a more detailed report than the homebuyer survey. It is recommended for older properties and those in need of work, or simply for peace of mind. Make sure that the person carrying out the survey is qualified to do so. You can find a qualified surveyor in the yellow pages or online.

This is suitable for properties which are large, more than 80 years old or in a poor condition. The Building Survey Report will give the current condition of the property and may recommend further tests or investigations, for example, a specialist checks for woodworm or damp. This is particularly suitable for properties built this century which appear reasonably sound. It is much cheaper than a full structural survey.

What if things go wrong?

You may find that the new home you have bought has a problem that you feel should have been discovered during the survey. If so, you should complain to the person or organisation that carried out the survey in writing. If you are not happy with the response, you should seek professional advice from a lawyer or Citizens Advice Bureau.

Warranties on New Properties

If you buy a property that is less than ten years old, it may be covered by a building warranty. The warranty is a guarantee that covers you if there are any defects that come to light and need fixing. The warranty provider may offer to fix or pay out money if certain defects or problems arise with the property. You should make sure you know what types of defects are covered by the warranty and which are not. The warranty will usually transfer to the new owner if you sell the property.

If the property is a newly-built property, check whether it has a Buildmark warranty. Buildmark warranties are organised by the National House-Building Council (NHBC) which is an independent organisation with over 20,000 builders of new houses on its register. Before being accepted onto the NHBC register, builders must be able to show that they are technically and financially competent and they must also agree to keep to NHBC Standards.

The Buildmark scheme covers homes built by NHBC registered builders once the NHBC has certified them as finished. The scheme will, for example, protect your money if the builder goes bankrupt after contracts have been exchanged but before completion. It also covers defects which arise because the builder has not kept to NHBC Standards.

If the surveyor reports that there are some problems with the property, you will have to consider whether you still want to go ahead with the purchase or want to negotiate further with the seller about the price. The surveyor will usually advise you as to how any problems they have identified should be dealt with and the likely costs of this.

Legal and Conveyancing Fees

You will need to hire a solicitor to deal with the legal aspects of buying a property. There is no standard fee so it is a good idea to shop around for the best rate. Some solicitors charge a flat rate while others charge a percentage of the property price, normally up to half a percent. As well as the price of your house, the fee will take into account factors such as the amount of paperwork involved, how much skill is required and how complicated the transaction is. You will also have to pay for the legal work done by your lender's solicitor. Again, prices vary so ask your lender how much they will charge. If you use the same solicitor as the lender to do your conveyancing this may save you money, but compare charges with other firms.

A solicitor or conveyancer will check all the ownership details, make sure the property is not subject to any planning actions and arrange the transfer of the price and details between the buyer, seller and lender. Legal fees may come to £3,500 normally, but you will also have to pay the additional expenses, such as Land Registry fees and the cost of searches.

Stamp Duty

This has changed significantly in recent months and years with helping first time buyers at the bottom of the ladder and taxing richer home buyers at the top. At the moment first time buyers only pay Stamp Duty on properties over £250,000 (until 24th March 2012) while, on 6 April this year (2011) homes bought for £1m and over will attract a 5% levy.

Below is the full Stamp Duty table:

Up to £125,000: **1%** (*except first time buyers, who pay nothing*).
From £125,001 to £250,000: 2% (*except first time buyers, who pay nothing*).
From £250,001 to £500,000: 3%.
From £500,001 to £1m: 4%.
Over £1m: 5%.

Disadvantaged Areas

If you are buying a residential property in an area designated by the government as a disadvantage area, you do not have pay any Stamp Duty Land Tax if the purchase price is £150,000 or less. For more information on this, go to the HM Revenue & Customs and seek clarification.

Land Registry Fee

The Land Registry is a government department, which looks after the registers of all registered properties in England and Wales. It charges a fee for transferring the register to the new owner. This fee is charged according to property price.

Price (£)	Fee (£)
Up to 40,000	40
40,001 - 70,000	60
70,001 - 100,000	100
100,001 - 200,000	200
200,001 - 500,000	300
500,001 - 1,000,000	500
1,000,001 and over	800

Mortgage Indemnity Guarantee (MIG)

This is an insurance premium charged by some lenders where your loan amount is more than 75% of the price of the property - in other words, where the loan to value (LTV) is greater than 75%.

A Mortgage Indemnity Guarantee, a higher lending charge is levied on borrowers who have relatively small deposits. Because their risk is considered greater, the charge is designed to offset any costs caused by default. Some lenders, no longer charge this fee to first time buyers. Some lenders only charge when the loan is more than 80% to 90%.

Contingency Fund

Leave a decent-sized contingency fund for emergencies. You do not want to be left completely penniless in case you have unexpected extra costs. Planning ahead can help you prepare for those expenses, and budget accordingly. Knowing in advance how your costs could add up will help you work out how much you can afford for your first home.

Other Costs

- Buildings insurance.
- Contents insurance.
- Installation of new equipment e.g. cable
- Carpet
- Travel expensive.
- Mail redirection.
- Search Fees.
- Estate Agents Fees.
- Removal Fees.
- Disconnection of services e.g. water, gas, electricity, telephone.
- Reconnection of services.

Decision time

If you have found the property that you like and is within your price range, ask to go and have a look at the place again, but without the pressure of the estate agent with you. This way you can take your time and view with a clear head. Try to picture the place with all your possessions in it, and if it feels like home then you can make an offer on the property, if not simply carry on looking at other property, until you find one that feels like home to you.

If you have been searching for a long time, it can be tempting to compromise your ideals and buy somewhere not altogether suitable, simply because you do not want to go and see any more property. Take stock and be certain that you are doing the right thing. If you have any doubts whatsoever, take some extra time to think it over. It is not fair on the seller to pull out halfway and it is not fair on yourself to end up in a place that you are not happy with. If you are sure and you know it is what you really want then go ahead, make an offer. But remember; just because you decide you want it, there is no guarantee that you will end up buying the place. A lot can still go wrong.

Making an offer

When you decide you would like to buy a particular property that you like, you do not necessarily have to pay the price being asked for it by the owners. You can offer less if, for example, you think that there are repairs to be done to the property which will cost you money. If you do not ask, you will never know what you might get. It could save you thousand of pounds if the seller lowers their asking price; you have got nothing to lose.

If the property is being sold through an Estate Agent, you should tell the Estate Agent what you are prepared to pay for the property. The Estate Agent will then put this offer to the owners, if the owners do not accept the first offer put to them by you; you can decide to increase the offer to the sellers. There is no limit on the number of times you can make offers on a property. If you make a written offer it will always be made subject to contract. This means that you will not be committed to the purchase before finding out more about the state of the property. If you make an oral offer this is never legally binding.

Estate Agent and making an offer

Estate Agents usually act on behalf of the seller, but must also treat buyers fairly. If you make an offer on a property, make sure that it is subject to contract. This means you can pull out of the deal if there are any problems. Under the Estate Agents Act, an Estate Agent is legally bound to present any offer promptly and in writing to the person selling the house, unless the seller has said in writing that there are some offers that they do not wish to receive.

A buyer's offer is not legally binding in England and Wales, even if it is accepted by the seller. This means that the Agent is legally obliged to pass on any other offer received for the property up to when contracts are exchanged.

Once your offer is accepted, ask for the property to be taken off the market for the duration of the sale. This is one step you can take to try to avoid being gazumped. The seller may be reluctant to do this if you have not already sold your property.

Making a Complaint

All Estate Agents must belong to redress schemes run by either The Property Ombudsman (TPO) or the Surveyors Ombudsman Service (SOS). Redress schemes will help you if you have a complaint about an Estate Agent.

When the offer has been accepted

When your offer for the property has been accepted you will have to consider the following:-

- Whether a holding deposit is payable.
- Arranging a mortgage.
- Whether a survey is necessary.
- Who will do the necessary legal work.
- Whether you want to buy with someone else.

Deposit

Once the owners have accepted your offer the buyer may be asked to pay a small deposit to the estate agent. This is usually between £500 and £1000. It is meant to show that you are serious about going ahead with the purchase. It is repayable if the sale does not go ahead.

Mortgage Arrangement

Most mortgage lenders require a deposit of at least five to ten per cent of the value of the property you wish to buy, as the price of property increases, the deposit can become expensive. You may want to consider asking family or friends for financial help. There are many types of mortgages available and some are targeted specifically at first time buyers.

If your income is not high enough to buy the sort of home you want, you could consider involving a parent. They may be as keen as you are to help you move out and could become a joint borrower or a guarantor for your mortgage. Alternatively you could pool resources and buy with a friend or partner, who could help you move or get a property of an appropriate size. Make sure you have a legal agreement in place to cover the costs, if something should happen in the near future and you both go your separate ways. This can be difficult to negotiate when you end on less than friendly terms.

If you have not already begun to arrange a mortgage, you should start to do this now. It should take about four weeks from the application for the mortgage to the formal offer being made by the lender. However, this timescale may vary. More on this part in the mortgage section of this book.

Whoever agrees to lend the money will want to have the property valued. This is to make sure that the lender could get the loan back if for any reason you stopped paying your mortgage and the house had to be sold again. The valuation will be done by a surveyor on behalf of the lender but you will have to pay for this valuation. The fee will be payable in advance, usually when you send a completed mortgage application form to the lender.

If the amount of money to be borrowed is more than a certain percentage of the valuation of the property (usually 75-80%), your lender may make it a condition of the loan that you take out extra insurance to cover the extra amount. You pay a single premium to your lender which is usually added to the loan. This is known as a higher lending charge or mortgage indemnity guarantee.

It is human nature to try to strike a deal, but if you find your ideal home and it seems to be priced correctly, consider offering the full asking price. This means you will be taken seriously, there will not be any time wasting and it will lessen the possibility of another party stepping in or gazumping you for the property. All offers should be made with the stipulation of taking the property off the market. Getting a Sold Board outside the property is a good way to stop others from looking to purchase the property. You might also want to ensure that all Internet adverts for the property have been removed, to prevent any further interest.

Gazumping

Gazumping is outbidding rivals at the last minute, to purchase a property. Estate Agents are powerless to stop this from ever happening even if they want to. In Scotland there are laws to protect the buyer from this taking place. Under the Estate Agency Act, Estate Agents are obliged to pass on all offers they receive, to the sellers, although some determined buyer will probably go straight to the sellers and make an offer for the property.

There is little you can do to stop a determined bidder from doing this with the present law that we have, but there are ways to lessen the chance of it happening, or at least reducing the impact if it do con about. Offer the full asking price and request that the property is removed from the market as soon as your offer is accepted. Be flexible with the seller and do not quibble over minor points in the property. Make it clear that you are willing to complete on their timescale, not yours.

First-time buyers

There are still some hopeful sign for the affordability for first time buyers in 2011 according to Halifax Buyers Review, with the present low interest rate and house price at a seven-year low from its peak of 2007. With over 95 per cent of first time buyers now do not have to pay stamp duty on their property. The main problem first time buyer's face is the tightening in lending by banks in its criteria to lend. In order for first time buyers to buy their property they have to have a very high deposit of between 20-25 per cent to purchase their property. The majority of first time buyers are now settling for terraced style property as they are cheaper and is the only way to get onto the property market, then moving up the ladder to semi-detached once their circumstances changed. The biggest obstacle at present is finding the large deposit that is now required by the banks to purchase your property, until the day comes when the banks lower its deposit requirement there will be a lot of angry people out there who want to purchase their own property rather than rent a property.

A recent survey by the Building Society Association found that over 59 per cent are willing to purchase a property now if it was not for the high deposit that the banks require from you together with the difficulty in lending criteria to get a mortgage now.

The ever-rising cost of housing has made it difficult for first-time buyers, so people are increasingly seeking alternative means of getting on the property ladder. Buying with your friends or family are two popular options, but you could also take part in a shared ownership scheme. This allows you to buy a percentage of your home, and pay rent on the remainder, with the option of increasing your share as and when you can afford it. Many of these homes are new-builds, with initial shares starting from around 25%, and the eventual option of owning the whole property.

Different housing authorities have different criteria for who can participate in shared-ownership schemes. To find out if you are eligible, take a look at the Communities and Local Government Advice website.

Buying a home for the first time can be expensive. Make sure you have an idea of the different costs and find out ways you could make buying a home possible and less daunting.

Buying with someone else

You may want to think about buying a home with other family members, friends or a partner. Buying with others can be a solution to coming up with the deposit and sharing costs. It is important to carefully think about what might happen if circumstances change and one of you want to sell their share of the property. You should get legal advice and draw up an agreement as to how property will be divided in case of death, or if one of you decide to give up their share in the property. You may choose to buy your property jointly with someone else, such as your husband, wife, civil partner, partner, relative or friend. If you buy your property with someone else, you can choose to do this in one of two ways, as either:

- Beneficial joint tenants
- Tenants in common

This is the case whether you own the freehold or leasehold of the property. If you are thinking about buying a property with someone else, you should get legal advice on the best type of ownership for you.

What if you simply do not have access to that kind of deposit many buyers need financial help from their parents to buy a home for the first time. You have a choice either wait to build up a larger deposit or considered a shared ownership purchase. Typically under such schemes, housing associations allow you to buy 25% of a property and rent the balance until you can afford to buy the rest of it in stages. The level of deposit required will come down and be closer to 5-10 % of a full purchase price.

Beneficial joint tenants

If you own your property as a beneficial joint tenant, this means that it belongs to you and the other owners jointly. You cannot re-mortgage or sell the property without the agreement of all the other owners. However if there is a dispute, an owner can apply for a court order.

As a beneficial joint tenant, you do not own specific shares in the property and you cannot give away a share of the property in a will. If you die, your interest in the property passes automatically to the other owners.

Tenants in common

If you own your property as tenants in common, this means that it belongs to you and the other owners jointly. This means that you all also own a specific share of it the value. It is up to you to decide how much each share will be.

You can give away, sell or mortgage your share. If you die, your share of the property does not pass automatically to the other owners. You can leave your share to who ever you like in your will.

Choosing who is going to do your legal work

Steps in the legal work of buying a property

Although it is impossible to give a precise idea of how long the legal work involved in buying a property takes, it is possible to offer guidelines. From having an offer accepted to exchange of contracts can take up to twelve weeks and from exchange of contracts to completion can take up to four weeks. However, if there are any problems the time taken may be longer.

Conveyancing is the process of legally transferring ownership of a property from the seller to the buyer. Conveyancing also includes the various searches and checks and any final tasks following the sale. Find out what happens at each stage and what you need to do as a buyer.

Once you have instructed your solicitor, in England and Wales, or a Conveyancer, the Seller's Solicitor or the Licensed Conveyancer draws up a contract which will eventually be signed by you and the Seller. However, before the contract can be signed, your solicitor or licensed conveyancer must make sure that there are no problems with the ownership of the property, rights of way, access, or future developments in the area that might affect the property. The legal process of transferring the ownership of the property from the present owner to the buyer is known as conveyancing. You should decide who you want to do the conveyancing work. You can do it yourself – although this can be complicated – or you can:-

- Use a solicitor; or
- Use a licensed conveyancer.

If you do not understand the legal implication of the property that you are buying then you are asking for a lot of problems as you will never know what is hidden in the property deeds until it is too late. As your property is going to be the biggest investment that you are likely to make, it is essential that you get this right first time and pay a property specialist solicitor to do the work for you as you may never know what he may find for example if you have purchased a property near a an old church, you may be liable for the repair of the church.

- This is known as a Chancel Repair Liability. This medieval law was for the cost of the church repairs being split between the parish and its parishioners. This old law has never changed over time to the present day. This normally occurs in rural areas where the church was at the centre of community life. The deed of your property will indicate if you have any liability to the church. The government has now stated that all chancel repairs obligations will cease from October 2013 unless the Church has noted their interest in your property.

- Other things to look out for are Restrictive Covenants, this is usually put in place by the owner of land and property before it is sold. This may restrict the new owner from building on the land or used for business activity.

- Footpath and right of way has been establish over many centuries and can run across people's property and land. As the owner of a property with a public footpath or right of way on it, you have to ensure that it is clearly marked and does not block or direct the footpath away even if it has not been used as this is illegal and can be very costly to have it moved.

- Shared Access is when you and your neighbour have a shared facility for example a driveway. Here you have certain rules to follow as to who owns the access, who is responsible for the maintenance.

Using a solicitor

Most firms of solicitors offer a conveyancing service. Although all solicitors can legally do conveyancing work, it is advisable to choose a solicitor who has experience of this type of work. You can use a licensed conveyancer to do your conveyancing work for you. Licensed Conveyancers are not solicitors but are licensed by the Council for Licensed Conveyancers. If you want to find out if a local conveyancer is licensed you can write to: The Council for Licensed Conveyancers

How much will it cost

Before making a choice as to who will do the Conveyancing work for you, you should be advised to find out the probable costs of the conveyancing. It is important to contact more than one solicitor or licensed conveyancer as there is no set scale of fees for conveyancing. You should:-

• Check whether the figure quoted is a fixed fee or depends on how much work is involved.
• Check that the figure includes stamp duty, search fees, land registration fees, expenses and VAT and get a breakdown of these costs find out what charges, if any, will be made if the sale falls through before contracts are exchanged.

Everyone buying or selling a property should employ a property solicitor also known as a conveyancer. The legal process of buying and selling property in England & Wales differs from the process in Scotland. The three main stages of conveyancing for a Buyer are:-

• Agreement of Sale.
• Exchange of contracts.
• Completion.

Buying a property in England & Wales

Stage 1 - Agreement of sale

You will need to make payments to the seller during the conveyancing process. If you hire a solicitor or licensed conveyancer, they may ask you for the money in advance so payments can be made without delay.

Once you have made an offer to buy a property, legal documents need to be prepared to transfer ownership from the seller to you. The seller draws up a contract for your agreement – you can negotiate its terms if necessary. If you have instructed a solicitor or licensed conveyancer, they will carry out this work and advise you on the contents of the contract.

The contract contains details including:-

- What the boundaries of the property are.
- What fixtures and fittings are included in the sale.
- Receive replies to questions raised and report to you with the contract for signing.
- Request your deposit.
- Receive the search results and communicate any problems.
- Any legal restrictions or rights on the property like any public footpaths or rules about use of the property.
- Deal with the formal mortgage offer and all the conditions on your behalf.
- Any planning restrictions in place.
- A description of the services to the property, e.g. Electricity and gas.
- The date for completing the purchase.

Other tasks to be done at this stage are explained below.

Before you sign and exchange the contract, both you and your solicitor or conveyancer should find out as much as possible about the property. The sellers do not have to voluntarily tell you about any problems there might be within the property or neighbourhood. The seller should, however, reply truthfully to enquiries. Your solicitor or licensed conveyancer will do a number of searches and checks including:

- Title check, this proves the seller's ownership.
- Asking the local authority about any planned works like roadwork's or new developments that might affect the property.
- Enquiries to the seller's solicitor or licensed conveyancer about the details of the contract.

Your solicitor or conveyancer may need to carry out additional searches depending on the type of property involved. For example, if your property is in an area where there have been mines, your solicitor or licensed conveyancer will need to do a mining check on the land.

Stage 2 - Exchange of contracts

When the buyer and seller are happy with its contents, they sign final copies of the contract and send them to each other. This is called the exchange of contracts. Once contracts are exchanged, the agreement to sell and buy is legally binding and usually neither party can pull out without paying compensation. Buyers will usually pay the seller a deposit usually 5-10 per cent of the purchase price of the property at the exchange of contracts stage.

In many cases, there are a few further checks to be done at this stage. After the exchange of contracts, if not dealt with already your solicitor or conveyancer will.

Once contracts have been exchanged, your solicitor will:-

- Check that you are satisfied with the final outcome of all the enquiries.
- Any surveyor's report has been received and any necessary action taken.
- The formal mortgage offer has been received.
- Arrangements about the payment of the 10% deposit have been made.
- The date of completion has been agreed.
- Prepare the legal documents to transfer ownership
- Check mortgage documents.
- Arrange for the transfer of funds to the seller.
- Organise final searches to check for debts and bankruptcy.

- Check all agreed tasks set out in the contract have been done, like agreed repairs.
- Check that fixtures and fittings have been left as agreed.
- Energy Performance Certificate Report has been done?

You and the seller will each have a copy of the final contract which you must sign. These signed contracts are then exchanged. At exchange of contracts both you and the seller are legally bound by the contract and the sale of the house has to go ahead. If you drop out, you are likely to lose your deposit. You should make arrangements for the supply of gas, electricity and telephone service and make sure that the seller is arranging for final meter readings to be made.

Stage 3 – Completion

Once all matters between exchange and completion have been dealt with, the money for the property is transferred from buyer to seller. The sale is now completed and the keys are handed over. The property now belongs to the buyer.

Completion of the purchase usually takes place about four weeks after exchange of contracts, although it can be earlier. Your solicitor or licensed conveyancer can advise you on how to pay the Land Registry fees and Stamp Duty. On the day agreed for completion:-

- The mortgage lender releases the money.
- The deeds to the property are handed over to your solicitor or licensed conveyancer.
- The seller must hand over the keys and leave the property by an agreed time.
- Pay the seller the remainder of the cost of the property through your solicitor or licensed conveyancer.

- Prepare and send off application to HM Land Registry to register your ownership of the property.
- Pay Stamp Duty Land Tax (Stamp Duty).
- Pay your solicitor's or licensed conveyancer's fees, if not already done.

The solicitor or licensed conveyancer (in England and Wales only) will usually send their account to you on, or soon after, the completion date.

Buying a property in Scotland

- Before an Offer.
- Making an Offer.
- Concluding an offer.

Stage 1 - Before an offer - your solicitor will:

- Contact the seller's agent notifying your interest in the property they may try to obtain an assurance that the property will not be sold once you have put in an offer.
- Confirm you have a loan in place sufficient to cover the expected offer.
- Arrange a survey for you, if necessary, and report the contents back to you.

Stage 2 - Making an offer - your solicitor will:

- Official letter, with the details of your offer and any conditions you have attached - for example, a time limit.
- Submit it to the agent marketing the property.
- Receive written confirmation from the seller's solicitor as to the acceptance, or not, of your offer.

- Act on your instructions as to accepting any of the alterations proposed and return a letter to the buyer's solicitor, this process may be repeated a number of times.

Stage 3 - Concluding an offer - your solicitor will:

- Acknowledge conclusion of the offer.
- Perform any necessary searches with relation to the property for sale.
- Prepare and send off application to HM Land Registry to register your ownership.
- Send the title deeds to the building society or bank (if the property is mortgaged).
- Receive and arrange for payment for the property to be sent to the seller's solicitor and for any stamp duty to HM Revenue & Customs.

Arranging to pay the deposit

Whilst the solicitor or, in England and Wales, a licensed conveyancer is making the enquiries, you should sort out how you will pay the deposit that has to be made when the contracts are exchanged. This deposit is often 5-10% of the price of the home but it can vary. Clearly this will depend on the price of the property you find, but for the most attractive rates you would need to put down 30% of the purchase price. The monthly charge will not be the only expense involved. The higher a loan as a percentage of the purchase price, the higher the interest rates will be. If you are also selling a house, it is usually possible to put the deposit on the property being sold towards the deposit on the property you are buying.

If raising the deposit is a problem, you could consider borrowing the money for the deposit from relatives or you could try to get a bridging loan from a bank. However, the amount of interest you will have to pay for a bridging loan will be high and you should check how much this arrangement will cost. Discuss your options with your solicitor or licensed conveyancer.

Insuring the property

You should make sure that buildings insurance is arranged from the date of exchange, because once contracts have been exchanged you are responsible for the property. You may be able to get information on buildings insurance from your mortgage lender, solicitor or, in England and Wales, a licensed conveyancer.

Property Tax

If you buy a property in the UK over a certain purchase price you have to pay Stamp Duty Land Tax (SDLT). This is charged on all purchases of houses, flats and other land and buildings.

Stamp Duty Land Tax (SDLT) has replaced the Stamp Duty Tax in December 2003. This tax is on the purchase price of land and buildings. For example when you buy a property or take on a lease you may have to pay SDLT.

Stamp Duty Land Tax

If you buy either a freehold or a leasehold property and the purchase price is more than £125,000, you pay SDLT of, between one and four per cent of the whole purchase price. See the table below for more detail. If the purchase price is £125,000 or less you don't pay any SDLT. The £125,000 threshold for when you start to pay SDLT was introduced again on 1 January 2010. The previous starting rate was £175,000 - for purchases made between 3 September 2008 and 31 December 2009.

First-time buyers

If you are a first-time buyer the threshold for when you start to pay SDLT is £250,000. This is only if you have never owned a house or flat in the UK or anywhere else in the world. If you are buying with someone else they must never have owned property before either. This higher threshold applies to purchases made on or after 25 March 2010 and before 25 March 2012.

Purchase price of residential property	Rate of SDLT (percentage of the total purchase price)	Rate of SDLT - first-time buyers (percentage of the total purchase price)
£0 - £125,000	0%	0%
£125,001 - £250,000	1%	0%
£250,001 - £500,000	3%	3%
£500,001 or more	4%	4%

You can check current rates of SDLT on the HM Revenue & Customs (HMRC) website.

As the buyer of the property, you are responsible for completing the land transaction return and paying the SDLT. However, in practice, your solicitor or licensed conveyancer will usually handle this for you and send it to HMRC on your behalf. You should check that all the information on the form is correct and complete before signing the declaration.

SDLT Disadvantaged Areas Relief

If you buy property in an area designated by the government as disadvantaged you may qualify for Disadvantaged Areas Relief. In this case the threshold for SDLT is £150,000. If you are a first-time buyer you don't need to apply as the threshold for first-time buyers is higher. Disadvantaged Areas Relief did not apply for residential property purchases between 3 September 2008 and 31 December 2009 inclusive. The threshold during that period was £175,000 which is higher than the previous Disadvantaged Areas Relief threshold. You can check the HMRC website to see if the property you are buying is in an area designated as disadvantaged.

Zero-Carbon Homes

In October 2007 a relief from SDLT was introduced for zero-carbon homes. All qualifying houses under £500,000 are exempt and houses bought for £500,000 or above will have their SDLT bill reduced by £15,000.
A zero-carbon home can be connected to mains electricity and gas but needs to have sufficient additional renewable power to cover the average consumption of a house over a year.

In order to achieve this, the fabric of the building has to be insulated and built to very high standards and the house needs to incorporate renewable energy technologies. The house must be zero-carbon over the course of the year.

CAPITAL GAINS TAX

The dream of owning a holiday home, in the country or by the sea, is likely to look considerably less attractive as the government begins to crack down on the tax advantages of owning furnished holiday lets. In its emergency Budget on 22 June, the new coalition government, much to the relief of many, reversed the previous government's decision to remove major tax benefits of owning furnished holiday lets. Yet on 27 July, it announced its own measures to ensure that the tax benefits are not abused, by proposing a dramatic increase in the number of days a home must be let in order to qualify. At present, a property only has to be available for letting for 140 days, and actually let for just 70 days in any given year, before the owner qualifies for beneficial tax treatment.

This includes:

- The ability to offset excess property expenses, including mortgage interest, against other income at the landlord's highest rate of income tax.
- A capital gains tax (CGT) rate of just 10% on profits realised on the sale of the property.
- The ability to defer CGT by reinvesting into new qualifying property, and to make gifts within the family without a CGT charge.

OUTLOOK FOR THE PROPERTY MARKET

With the UK mortgage market at very low levels, how does this affect different groups of people looking to move home? What can they do to improve their chances of getting the mortgage and home they want? A social divide is likely to widen owing to difficulties in securing a mortgage without access to a large deposit. Young first-time buyers who get financial help from their parents are much more likely to get on the property ladder. More mortgages with a deposit of less than 25% are available now, than was the case a year ago. The bigger the deposit, the more competitive the rates will be.

This means that there is less pressure on buyers to put in an offer quickly, fearing that the price would keep going up if they delay for a few months. The increasing numbers of properties coming on to the market mean first-time buyers can haggle on prices. Buyers can look seriously at two or three properties, rather than setting their heart on one, which might be overpriced.

As with first-time buyers, it is important for them to maintain a good credit score in order to secure a competitive mortgage. Lenders may now also ask for the last three months of bank statements, so high spending might be better put on a credit card and then paid off immediately, rather than on a debit card where the spending is obvious to the lender. Ensuring all bills are paid on time, making sure they are on the electoral roll, and not regularly switching and closing bank accounts would also help to keep a good credit score.

It is worthwhile looking at the trend in prices where you are looking to move to, and making a judgement. However, over time, prices do tend to catch up in areas that have lagged behind the national average, or slow down when prices have been over-inflated. It is worthwhile looking at the trend in prices where you are looking to move to, and making a judgement. People often do not do enough homework on the local market because of the distances involved in searching for properties somewhere new. Meanwhile, the self-employed face a further hurdle of mortgage lenders' doubts over giving home loans to those with a variable income.

Below is a quick reference guide as to what is needed to make the buying process quick and trouble free.

The Buying Process: A Step-by-Step Guide

The main stages you will go through when buying a home.

- Work out how much you can afford.
- Get a mortgage agreement in place.
- Find your home.
- Find a Solicitor.
- Make an Offer.
- Have a Survey and Valuation done on the property.
- Finalise Your Mortgage.
- Exchange Contract on the property.
- Insurance arrange for the property.
- Make arrangement for moving day.
- Finalise the contract details.
- Move In.

"Enjoy your new home"

3. OTHER TYPES OF PROPERTIES TO BUY

HOW TO BUY A NEW BUILD HOUSE OR FLAT

If you are buying a newly built home, please make sure that it is covered by a good warranty to cover you if there are problems with the building in the future.

If you are looking to buy a new-build home, there are certainly plenty of advantages. New Homes tend to be more energy-efficient than older properties, they may include the latest fixtures and fittings and, of course, they are chain-free, allowing for a quicker purchase. Many house-builders also offer generous financial incentives for prospective buyers. With a new built property you also have peace of mind from its warranty if things go wrong.

With the recent cold weather new build property are becoming very popular to purchase with all its energy efficiency compared to the older type property that are less energy efficient. If last December is any thing to go by, the demand for this type of property will be increasing significantly due to its energy saving within the property. With prices on the increase the cost of upgrading an older property is very expensive, so buying an energy efficient property is very cost effective both in the short term and long term because of the ever increasing energy price.

But there are other things to consider as well, such as choosing the right property developer and conducting adequate property inspections. Below gives a general guide of the things you should look out for, and find out how well the property meets environmental standards.

Advantages of buying a new home

Buying a new-build property can be a very exciting and practical way to create a ready-made home. You can view thousands of new-build houses and apartments from the UK's leading property developers on their websites.

Energy efficiency

Modern building regulations dictate that house-builders meet certain standards regarding the energy efficiency of homes, making them more environmentally sound and also saving the homeowner money on bills. These features include:-

- High quality insulation throughout the walls, roof and floor
- Energy-efficient central heating systems
- Double glazing
- Energy-efficient light bulbs, regulations in England & Wales require at least two rooms are fitted with energy efficient light bulb fittings to take low wattage bulbs.
- Better draught-proofing.

Financial incentives

Financial incentives are often on offer for buyers and this makes new homes particularly attractive for first time buyers struggling to get their foot on the ladder. Such incentives might include all or a proportion of the deposit paid for by the developer, or your stamp duty paid on your behalf. Also developers will purchase your old home at market value, based on an independent survey valuation report. No need to sell your property in the traditional way. This incentive means all the hard work is done for you.

Location

Builders know that location is one of the most important considerations for buyers and are very careful about developing on land that is close to all the local amenities, such as schools, doctors, shopping facilities and transport terminals. Search for new-build homes for sale to check out the local amenities and facilities available in a particular area.

Security and fixtures and fittings

The latest building regulations require that adequate security and safety features are built into the specifications of the property. These will most likely include smoke and burglar alarms.

Most new homes come with the latest fixtures and fittings to attract a purchase. These might include a fully fitted kitchen, carpets, bathrooms and toilets with all the latest mod-cons. Many also come with en suite facilities for at least the master bedroom.

Chain-free purchase

Being brand new and with no inhabitants, there is no chain to worry about. This means transactions can happen more quickly and you aren't delayed in making your move. A new-build home is essentially a blank canvas for you to make your own mark upon. Although the basics will be in place and some neutral decoration will have been undertaken, you will usually have the option to fit out the property to your own taste.

NHBC Certificate

Make sure that the property is protected by a good warranty, guarantee provided by a reputable company. All builders that are members of the National House-Building Council (NHBC) will provide a ten year warranty and insurance policy on the property to safeguard you against any major problems with the building and to give you peace of mind. However some builders use other warranty providers and can give you full details of the property's warranty. You should ensure that the final building control certificate is available if the new property is not covered by an NHBC or similar warranty. Take time to understand the cover provided by your warranty.

Find a House-Builder

When looking for a new-build house, check that any builders you come across are members of the National House-Building Council (NHBC). Members of the NHBC must maintain the building standards and rules set by the Council and should give you confidence that the property is built to a high quality. The NHBC will inspect the property to check that standards are being maintained during construction. Check that the builder has a good reputation. Visit the site; if it is tidy and well managed, this will give you information about the builder's commitment to quality. Conduct your own research on the house-builder to make sure you are satisfied with their quality. This might include:-

- Visiting the site to see how it is being managed
- Seeing if residents already in the development are happy with the quality of the product
- Searching the Internet for information and feedback on your builder
- Family or Friends who recently purchase a new build home.

Code for Sustainable Home.

All new homes in England now have to have a compulsory rating. This rating lets you know how well your home meets environmental standards. The code helps homebuyers get better information about the impact of their new home on the environment, and its potential running costs.

Negotiate with the house-builder

You will have the chance to negotiate the price of the property with the builder and your success will often depend on whether there are homes that have remained unsold for longer than expected. If the builder has targets to achieve and the properties need to be sold sooner rather than later, you may just be able to negotiate a better price. You should also remember that there will be other angles for negotiation, such as promotional deals on mortgages or payment of stamp duty. See if you can negotiate extras into the deal, such as flooring, curtains, having the garden landscaped, many will not include a finished garden with the property.

Show homes

Most developments will include a show home. It is the developer's opportunity to 'sell' the property to you, and the property will often be decorated to the highest standard. However, the show home may be different from the property you're interested in, so make sure you get the opportunity to see the actual property you intend to buy if it is in a suitable state of development. Be sure to clarify what is included in the property, as most show homes will have the extras that do not usually form part of the sale.

Choose a solicitor that has experience of new-build homes

It is often advisable to instruct a solicitor that has experience of managing the purchase of new-build properties. If possible, try to use an independently selected solicitor, rather than one recommended by the builder. You can find a solicitor from the law solicitors' websites.

Inspect the property

Before the legal completion date, make sure you conduct a thorough inspection of the property to identify any problems that need addressing. Remember, you are paying a lot of money for the property, so it is in your interest to make sure you're getting a high-quality product. After the first six months of living in your property, conduct another inspection, or note down any problems with the property since you've been living there and notify the developer in writing. Your builders are obliged to fix problems identified within the first two years of completion, otherwise the NHBC will. Normal issues, such as shrinkage and drying out, are not covered by the warranty.

After Exchange

- Once you have exchanged contracts:
- Get the warranty documents from your solicitor and read them carefully.
- Before taking possession of your home, make sure you inspect it carefully for any defects.
- Wait until the home is fully completed before you move in; once you have moved in, check your new home again thoroughly.

- Report any defects in writing to your builder and make sure you keep a copy.
- If you are in dispute with your builder, write to the appropriate NHBC office, if registered under the scheme.
- Consider getting a structural survey done, especially if your home is more than two years old.

AUCTION PROPERTY

Buying a property at auction is very different from the more conventional buying process. The property might be a repossessed house or flat, or could be in a state of disrepair. Success in buying a property at auction, including how to locate auction properties, the financial arrangements involved, what to expect on the day of the auction, and much more. It avoids all of the normal lengthy purchasing procedures that you usually have to endure, with the risk of everything falling through at the last minute.

With an auction, as soon as the hammer falls, that is it, the property is yours. However, it is not something to be undertaken lightly, and it definitely pays to have done some research on the process, in order to be in a position to snap up a potential bargain.

Auction preparation

The main attraction of buying at auction is that you avoid the conventional drawn out process of house buying. At auction it is all over within a matter of few minutes rather than months and when the hammer falls, you own the property.

- Contact the relevant auction house and request their catalogue. Most auction houses hold regular auction sales with a catalogue printed some weeks in advance. You can also subscribe to catalogue mailing lists.
- Go through the catalogue carefully, read the details thoroughly and identify the properties you are interested in.
- View any properties you are interested in.
- Carry out the usual property/land searches.
- Carefully read the conditions printed in the catalogue. Always get legal or professional advice from a solicitor and, in appropriate cases, a chartered surveyor.
- Make financial arrangements to ensure you have a 10% deposit ready for payment on auction day, when the contracts are signed and access to the remaining 90% within 28 days.
- Plan ahead if you need mortgage assistance. It is wise to arrange a mortgage in principal with a bank or building society before buying at auction. You could lose your 10% deposit if you fail to complete within the time given normally within 20 working days.
- Be aware that buying at auction is a binding commitment and carries the same legal implications as a signed contract by private treaty. In most cases, auction offices have copies of legal documentation provided by the seller's solicitors, which can be sent to you.

If you are considering purchasing a property at auction you should always consult with auction professionals and solicitors.

Day of the Auction

If you are unable to attend the auction, you can make a bid by telephone or in writing. Contact the auction house for more information:

- Remember to take two forms of identification, chequebook and all your banking details with you to the auction.
- On arrival, you may need to register with the auction house in order to bid prior to the start of the auction. Check with your auctioneer.
- Take a seat or stand somewhere in the room where the auctioneer will able to see you bidding clearly.
- When placing a bid, make sure you gesture clearly at the auctioneer. Subtle twitches and winks will not be picked up. Either raise your hand or nod/shake your head clearly. The auctioneer will warn the room when he is concluding a sale.
- Do not forget that the property becomes the buyer's insurable risk as soon as the hammer falls. The conditions assume that the buyer has acted like a prudent buyer. If you choose to buy a lot without taking these normal precautions you do so at your own risk.

The Auctioneer

Decide on your maximum bid in advance and be strict. If you do not trust yourself not to get carried away, have someone else bid on your behalf: -

- The auctioneer acts as an agent for each seller. They prepare the catalogue from information supplied by or on behalf of each seller. They will usually have a photograph of the property, a brief description and a guide price.

- The auctioneer sells each lot at the auction. During the auction, their decision on the conduct of the auction is final; they can cancel the auction, withdraw lots from sale, or alter the order in which lots are offered for sale.
- The auctioneer looks for bids around the room, and will take bids until there are no more and, depending on whether the reserve price has been met, will sell the property to the highest bidder. This sale is confirmed when the auctioneers hammer falls on the highest bid. At this point the successful bidder is immediately under a binding contract.
- If there is a dispute over bidding they are entitled to resolve it and their decision is final.

Likewise, acting as agents, the auctioneers can take offers placed by bidders before the day of auction to the seller and the seller may decide to sell before the auction. There are so many things to consider when viewing a property and often the most important questions are forgotten. Ensure you ask the relevant questions by taking our handy viewing checklist with you on your viewing.

When you have found the place of your dreams, your offer has been accepted and you are just waiting for the legal paperwork to be cleared. Although solicitors and estate agents carry out most of the work, it pays to keep a track of each stage of the purchase. The cost of buying a home can quickly mount up, leaving you wondering where all the money has gone.

Cost involved

- What's the maximum deposit I can put down?
- What's the maximum mortgage I can get?

- Estate agent's fee.
- Conveyancer's fee.
- Surveyor's fee.
- Lenders fee.
- Local authority search.
- Land registry Estimate.
- Stamp duty.
- Removal firms.
- Home improvements.
- Telephone, new line and transfer of old number.
- Mail redirection.
- Energy Performance Certificate (EPC).
- Emergency fund.

Locating a property auction

You will first need to find out when and where there is an auction in your local area. You can do this by scouring the property papers and magazines, or by speaking direct to the relevant estate agents.

Finding the right property

Once you have found an auction, the next essential thing to do is to request a catalogue, as you will need to study it thoroughly to see if there's something that takes your fancy. It is always better to be prepared.

Make sure that you do your research thoroughly, and compare the price and condition of the property to others that are similar, that might be on sale with local Estate Agents. You will very often find that the guide price of auction properties is set relatively low in order to attract bidders, so have in your mind what you think the true market value of the property is, and bid accordingly.

When you express an interest in a property to the auctioneers, there are usually available documentations relating to the property. You should read this thoroughly to see if it contains any covenants or certain legalities which could have potential implications on the value of the property. If you have any concerns about the property seek legal advice.

With the popularity of Auction House today, it should not be considered to that selling property this way is the last resort by sellers. A sale by auction has many advantages over the more traditional methods of selling, because it is faster, prices can be as good as selling through an Agents. It is all over in a matters of a few minutes, cost saving. Exchange of contract completed in 28 days. One of the benefits of auction buying is that from the sellers point of view is that any one who is bidding for their property has already had there 10 per cent deposit in place, and the balance of there finance within 28 days from the date of auction.

Viewing properties

Once you have identified any properties that you are interested in, then contact the auctioneers and arrange a viewing. As when buying any property, I would advise more than one viewing as you need to be aware of every detail of the property if you are considering bidding. Very often, auction properties are in a pretty poor state, so it could be advisable to take a builder or an architect with you to ascertain what can be done to the property, and how much it is likely to cost.

There is usually only a matter of around four weeks between the publication of the auction catalogue and the auction itself, so you have to act fast.

Arranging your finances

You will also need to make your financial arrangements prior to auction. You must have a ten percent deposit with you on auction day, and you must come up with the remaining ninety percent within twenty eight days. If you need a mortgage, it is prudent to have discussed all of the financial implications with a bank or building society, and have arranged a mortgage in principle. Make sure that your finance are in place before you bid, if not you will loose your deposit as well as the property itself.

The property auction

When you arrive at the auction, you will need to register, make sure that you bring identification and enough funds for your ten percent. Auction houses can be pretty crowded affairs, so get there early if you want a seat! When the time comes to bid, make sure that you can be seen by the auctioneer and that he is aware of when you are bidding.

Bidding

It can be very tempting to go over budget, when the time comes for the actual auction, be prepared. As the bidding increases, so will your heart rate, believe me. Have a figure in mind that you will not want go over. You do not actually have to be there in person, as you can bid by telephone. But the fun part is actually being at the Auction itself, with a room full of people all trying to out bid each other for the property that they want for themselves at a bargain price. Do your homework and only bid for a property that you want for yourself. Do not get carried away and bid for a property that you have not done any research on, as this can be a very risky price to pay for a property that needs a great deal of work to it.

If you are bidding on a property and it fails to meet its reserve price, this do not necessarily mean that this is the end of the matter. The auctioneers can still act as agents and are able to do a deal between yourselves and the sellers, if a price can be agreed at the end of the lot. This is often a good way to pick up a bargain, as a seller might have been chancing their arm with their reserve price, but could be willing to do a deal after the auction. Likewise, it is not unheard of for a deal to be tied up prior to the auction taking place, so it may be worthwhile checking this possibility out with the auctioneers.

Search for property for sale at Auction

If you are keen to buying a property at auction yourself, start by searching for auction property on various websites and local property auction houses.

The right to buy and the Statutory House Sales Scheme

To qualify, you must also have been a secure tenant of a social housing landlord for at least two years or in some cases five years.

As a tenant, you will not have the right to buy if you are:-

- A tenant of a property owned by a charity, although you may be entitled to a lump sum grant to help you buy on the open market.
- A tenant of sheltered housing or housing specifically designated for older people.
- An undercharged bankrupt. If you have rent arrears, you can still apply for the right to buy but you need to clear the arrears before the sale can go ahead.

Some assured tenants have what is called the preserved right to buy. You may have the preserved right to buy if the local authority sold your home to another landlord, for example, a housing association, while you were renting it. Your landlord can tell you if you have the preserved right to buy.

If you are not sure whether you have the right to buy, you should check with your landlord which category you fit into. If you are a secure tenant of a local authority, you should be given written information to help you decide about the right to buy.

At the present time we are not meeting the Government target requirement for building new homes. This has created a vast problem, and has therefore resulted in a long waiting list for Social Housing making it more difficult to purchase your own property.

Discounts

As a tenant with a right to buy, you will get a discount on the price of the property. If you live in a house the discount will be between 32% and 60%, depending on how long you have lived there. If you live in a flat, the discount will be between 44% and 70%, depending on how long you have lived there. The discount will not exceed the regional upper limits, which, in England and Wales, range from £16,000 to £38,000.

If you exercise the right to buy and then sell the property within a certain period, you may have to repay some or the entire discount. Check the rules with your local authority.

How to pay

As a tenant who wants to exercise your right to buy, you should try to obtain a mortgage from a building society or high street bank. You could also contact a mortgage broker to see if they can arrange a mortgage.

However, if you cannot afford to buy the property outright you can still buy under the rent to mortgage scheme. Under this scheme you can buy a share of the property and make mortgage repayments on the amount you have borrowed for this. The landlord will retain ownership of the remaining share of the property.

The right to acquire (England and Wales only)

As a secure or assured tenant of a social landlord, for example, a housing association or a local housing company, you may have the right to buy your home under a different scheme called the right to acquire. The right to acquire only applies to a limited number of properties, for example, homes built with public funds on or after 1 April 1997.

The Welsh Assembly Government has announced that in 2011 it will make it possible for local authorities in Wales to suspend the right to acquire in areas of housing pressure. This means that if you are a social housing tenant in Wales and want to buy your home at some time in the future, you may find you are no longer allowed to do so.

Shared ownership

Shared ownership schemes are intended to help people who cannot afford to buy a suitable home in any other way. You usually share ownership of the property with a local authority or housing association. You pay rent to the landlord for part of the property and a mortgage on the rest. You will usually be able to buy further shares in the property at a later date. If you can not afford to buy your first home, there are government schemes in England that can help. Find out what low-cost home ownership schemes are available and if you qualify to buy a home this way.

To qualify for the scheme you must usually be a first time buyer, and priority is given to local authority or housing association tenants. Other people in housing need may also be considered for the scheme. You must be able to get your own mortgage to meet the purchase costs on a percentage of the property.

First Buy Scheme

With the recent March Budget, a new £250million scheme called First Buy was announced to help the property market. The problem here is that only one part of the property market that will benefit is going to be the construction industry because the scheme is only available to purchasers of new homes. The problem here is that First Time Buyer, buying a new home, does not help the broader property market because their purchases do not affect the rotation of properties from buyers and sellers. Buyers and sellers of older type properties will still have the problems of selling and buying properties; this means a slower housing recovery. The numbers of buyers that this scheme will help is also very limited in numbers. This scheme is also limited for a period of a year.

This is just a window dressing of the Labour government's HomeBuy Direct scheme, which helped an extra 10,000 into home ownership but it is still not enough. With high prices and a difficult mortgage market mean there are at least 50,000 first time buyers being locked out of the housing market each year.

Low-cost home ownership schemes for newly build homes

If you live in England and cannot afford to buy a flat or house, you may get financial help to buy a home. There are two HomeBuy schemes to help people buy newly built homes:-

- HomeBuy Direct, you get a loan towards the home's purchase price that has no fees for five years.
- Shared ownership, you buy a share of your home and pay rent on the remaining share.

You will need to take out a mortgage to pay for your share of the home's purchase price. HomeBuy schemes are a first step to fully owning your home. When you can afford it, you can pay more money, for example, through savings or your mortgage, to own your home outright.

Shared Ownership for the Elderly

If you are aged 55 or over, you can get help from another HomeBuy scheme called Shared Ownership for the Elderly. It works in the same way as the shared ownership scheme, but you can only buy up to 75 per cent of your home. Once you own 75 per cent of the home, you won't have to pay rent on the remaining share.

HomeBuy Agents

HomeBuy schemes are run by local HomeBuy Agents, who have details of all the homes for sale through each scheme. HomeBuy Agents are housing associations that have been authorised to run schemes for people who have difficulty buying a home. If you want to buy a HomeBuy property, you will need to apply to the HomeBuy Agent for the area where you want to live.

Who can apply for the HomeBuy schemes

HomeBuy schemes are only open to households that earn £60,000 a year or less. A household is the number of people who are buying the home. For e.g., a household might be:-

- You alone.
- You and your partner.
- You and a friend.

HomeBuy schemes are open to:

People who rent council or housing association properties other schemes for tenants below:-

- Key workers in the public sector, for example, teachers, who work in the area.
- First-time buyers, you are a first-time buyer if you haven not owned a home before.

You can also get help through the HomeBuy schemes if you used to own a home, but can't afford to buy one now.

Rent to Homebuy

I am not going to say too much about this area as we are more concerned with purchasing our home and not renting it. If you cannot afford to buy a home through one of the HomeBuy schemes, you could qualify for 'Rent to HomeBuy'. With this scheme you rent a newly built property for up to five years and pay a reduced rent. This gives you the chance to save for a cash deposit so you can apply to buy a share of the home later. Contact the HomeBuy agent in your area if you want to apply for Rent to HomeBuy.

Low-cost home ownership schemes for people with disabilities

If you have a long-term disability, Home Ownership for People with Long Term Disabilities (HOLD) can help you buy any home that is for sale. You can only apply for HOLD if the homes in the other HomeBuy schemes do not meet your needs, for example you need a ground floor property. HOLD is a shared-ownership scheme: you buy a share of your home and pay rent on the remaining share.

Low-cost home ownership schemes for council and housing association homes

If you are a council or housing association tenant, there are three schemes to help you buy your home at a discount:-

- Right to Buy gives some council tenants the right to buy their rented home.
- Right to Acquire gives some housing association tenants the right to buy their rented home.
- Social HomeBuy gives some tenants the chance to buy a share of their council or housing association home.

These schemes are run by your landlord, for example, your council or housing association.

Find a HomeBuy Agent

If you can not afford to buy your first home, there are government schemes run by HomeBuy Agents that can help. Find out how to contact a HomeBuy Agent, including the National HomeBuy Agent once you've bought your home.

What HomeBuy Agents do

HomeBuy Agents are housing associations that have been authorised to run schemes for people who have difficulty buying a home.

They run HomeBuy schemes such as:-

- HomeBuy Direct - you can get a loan towards the home's purchase price that has no fees for five years.
- Shared ownership - you buy a share of the home and pay rent on the remaining share.

Your local HomeBuy Agent will:-

- Keep information about HomeBuy schemes on its website.
- Have information about all the properties in the area that you can buy through each HomeBuy scheme.
- Decide if you qualify for a scheme and handle your application.
- Pass on your application to other housing associations that may have properties for sale.

Find your local HomeBuy Agent

If you would like to buy a home through a HomeBuy scheme, you need to contact the HomeBuy Agent in the area where you want to live. Each HomeBuy Agent has an application form for each scheme, which you will need to complete.

The HomeBuy Agent can be found throughout the region for e.g., London, North East, South East Midlands. Find out from your Local Council Authority where your Agent is. For example, Orbit is the HomeBuy Agent for Birmingham, West Midlands.

National HomeBuy Agent

Once you have bought your home through the HomeBuy Direct scheme, you will deal with the National HomeBuy Agent. The National HomeBuy Agent is responsible for:-

- Collecting fees on your loan.
- Agreeing costs if you want to pay back the loan early.
- Approving the sale price of your home when you come to sell it.
- Collecting payment of the loan when you sell your home.

Metropolitan Home Ownership is the National HomeBuy Agent. Once you have bought your home through shared ownership, you will deal with the housing association that owns the other share of your home. This may not be the HomeBuy agent you applied to for the scheme.

Key Worker

Key workers are people who work in certain public sector jobs, like NHS clinical staff, who are eligible for help to buy a home. Find out whether you qualify as a key worker.

Who is eligible to buy a home as a Key Worker?

Key workers have certain public sector jobs based in England. You may be eligible for help to buy a home through one of the HomeBuy schemes if you are a key worker and you:

- Have a household income of £60,000 or less per year
- Are a first-time buyer.
- Are unable to afford to buy a property that meets your household's needs without help.
- Are a homeowner who needs to buy a larger property to meet your household's needs, for e.g. a family-sized home.

To buy a home as a key worker, one member of your household needs to be working in one of the following roles:

- Clinical NHS staff except for doctors and dentists.
- Teachers and nursery nurses in schools and further education or sixth form colleges.
- Police officers, community support officers and some civilian staff.
- Prison officers and some other prison staff.
- Probation Service staff.
- Planners working in a local authority.
- Firefighters and some other uniformed staff in Fire and Rescue Services.
- Armed Forces personnel and Ministry of Defence clerical staff, Ministry of Defence police officers and uniformed staff in the Fire and Defence Service.
- Qualified environmental health officers/practitioners who work in a local authority, government agency, the NHS or other public sector agencies.
- Highways Agency staff in certain safety roles in the traffic officer service.

- Social workers, nursery nurses, educational psychologists and therapists for example, occupational therapists employed by local authorities, the Children and Family Court Advisory Support Service or the NHS.

For more detailed information about the eligibility criteria for key workers, contact the HomeBuy Agent for the area where you want to live.

Buying your Council or Housing Association Home

If you are a council or housing association tenant, there are government schemes in place to help you buy your home. You can use Right to Buy and Right to Acquire to buy your home at a discount. You need to have been a tenant for at least five years. You may be able to buy the home you rent from your council at a discount under the Right to Buy scheme. Find out if you can buy your home through the scheme and what discount you could get.

If you rent a property from a housing association you may be able to buy your home at a discount. The scheme is called the Right to Acquire. Find out about the scheme and if you qualify for it.

Buying your home

You can use the Right to Buy and Right to Acquire Scheme to buy your home at a discount on its market value. This means you will get it for a lower price than it would fetch on the housing market.

You could qualify for Right to Buy if you:-

- Are a council housing tenant.

- Used to be a council housing tenant but your council home was sold to a housing association.

You could qualify for Right to Acquire if you are a tenant of a housing association. If you do not qualify for these schemes, or can not afford them, you could use the Social HomeBuy scheme. You can buy a share of your home and pay rent on the rest.

You can only apply for Right to Buy, Right to Acquire or Social HomeBuy if you have been a council tenant or public sector tenant for at least five years; you do not have to live their five years in a row. You are a public sector tenant if you have lived in properties provided by a housing association, the armed services or a public body like an NHS trust.

The Right to Buy Scheme

Right to Buy gives you a discount on the market value of your council home. The longer you have been a tenant the more discount you will get, up to a limit that depends on where you live. Sometimes you can not use Right to Buy scheme. For example, if you do not qualify for your home is sheltered housing for the elderly, the disabled or the mentally ill. To apply for Right to Buy, speak to your landlord. They will tell you if you qualify and will explain how you can apply.

If you are a tenant of a housing association, you can use the Right to Acquire to buy your home. Not all housing association homes are covered by Right to Acquire. Check with your landlord if you can buy your home through this scheme.

Right to Acquire gives you a discount between £9,000 and £16,000 on the value of your home. The discount you will get depends on where you live. Sometimes you can not use Right to

Acquire. For example, you will not qualify if you are bankrupt or you have been told by the court you must leave your home. To apply for Right to Acquire, speak to your landlord. They will tell you if you can buy your home through the scheme and will explain how you can apply.

Once you have bought your home, you will be responsible for the maintenance, repairs and repayments on a loan or mortgage. You will no longer qualify for certain benefits, for example housing benefit.

If you want to buy your home through Right to Buy, you will need to complete an application form and send it to your landlord. The Right to Buy scheme helps social tenants in England and Wales buy their council home at a discount. The scheme is open to people who are secure tenants, usually someone who has been a council tenant for more than 12 months.

You can apply for Right to Buy if you have been a council or public sector tenant for five years, it does not have to be five years in a row. You are a public sector tenant if you have lived in properties provided by a housing association, the armed services or a public body like an NHS trust. You can make a joint application to buy your home through Right to Buy with someone who shares the tenancy with you or with members of your family. They must have lived with you for the past 12 months.

The property you live in

To qualify for the Right to Acquire scheme, your property must either have been built or bought by a housing association with public funds from 1 April 1997 onwards, and transferred from a local council to a housing association after 1 April 1997. You can only buy your home through the scheme if your landlord is a housing association or housing company registered with the Tenant Services Authority. The Tenant Services Authority regulates landlords who provide social housing. The home you want to buy must also be a self-contained property and be your only or main home. Self-contained means you do not share parts of your property with others for example such as a living room or bathroom.

Who cannot buy under Right to Buy?

You can not buy through the scheme if:-

- The property is not your main home.
- The property is not self-contained or has a shared kitchen or bathroom.
- There is a court order saying you must leave your home.
- You are an undischarged bankrupt, for example you can not borrow money.
- You are being declared bankrupt.
- You owe money to creditors.
- Some properties will not be sold through Right to Buy, for example, if your home is suitable for housing the elderly.

Appealing if refused the Right to Buy

If your Right to Buy application is turned down by your landlord because the property is suitable for the elderly, you might be able to appeal to the Residential Property Tribunal.

Types of property that do not qualify for Right to Buy

Not all properties can be bought under the Right to Acquire scheme. These include:-

- Housing provided for people aged 60 or over.
- Housing provided to people who have special needs or who are physically disabled.
- Housing that is provided as part of your job.
- Property your landlord has published its intention to demolish within seven years.
- Property your landlord has served a notice to demolish within two years.
- There are other types of property that do not qualify for Right to Acquire. Your landlord will tell you if your home qualifies when you apply to buy it.

Right to Buyers discounts

If you qualify for Right to Buy, you can get a discount on the market value of your home when you buy it. Your home's market value is the price it would fetch if it was sold.

The discount is based on:-

- How long you have been a tenant.
- Where you live, the type of property you are buying for example a flat or a house.

If you have previously had a discount to help you buy a council home, this may be taken off your Right to Buy discount.

Mortgages and others costs of buying through a Right to Buy

Unless you can buy your home with cash, you will need to borrow money through a mortgage.

Make sure you will have enough money to pay your mortgage each month and other bills like Council Tax. If you buy a Flat, you will probably also have to pay a service charge towards the upkeep of the whole building and repairs. If major repairs are needed, for example a new roof, the service charge could be thousands of pounds each year. If you do not pay your mortgage, your mortgage lender can take you to court and you could lose your home, because you are no longer a tenant of the council, they do not have to find you another home.

Selling your Right to Buy home

If you sell your property within ten years of buying it, you must first offer it to your old landlord, for example, the council, or another social landlord in the area. Your home should be offered at the full sale price, which must be agreed between you and the landlord. If you can't agree on the price for your home, a district valuer will say how much your home is worth and set the price. You will not have to pay for their valuation.

If the landlords do not agree to buy your home within eight weeks, you can sell your home to anyone on the open market.

If you sell your home in the future you may have to repay some, or all, of the discount. The amount you'll have to pay back depends on how soon you want to sell your home.

4. SELLING A PROPERTY

There are many different reasons why people put their property on the market. Too many to list here, but generally it is because their family size is growing and they need a larger property, children schooling, to move up the housing ladder to a larger property, down sizing. It could be a job move or for family reasons such as a death, divorce or separation, or it could simply be a matter of wanting a different lifestyle in another part of the country, a more rural part of the country rather than a city lifestyle.

Each year 900,000 property sellers are unable to get a quick house sale or sell at all. On average, 1.8 million house sales are successful but data from the Government's Land Registry shows that 1 in 3 home sales fail. Add to this a widespread lack of confidence in UK Estate Agents and we think it's easy to see why selling a house and moving home has gained the reputation from being one of life's most stressful events. When you are ready to sell your property, one of the first things that you will need to do is organise yourself and set a time frame as to when and where you would like to move.

 Tidy up as much as possible and redecorate your property so that it looks clean and not outdated, even if you have to hire a skip to make the cleaning up process a lot easier; do it. This way you get rid of all unwanted items that you do not need. For example, children's toys, old books and tapes, the lists go on here. I hope you can see the point I am trying to make. Doing this will make the selling of your property a lot quicker, also with the valuation of the property it may make a difference of a few thousands pounds to your property. You have to look at this from the point of the purchaser.

- Will they like the look and style of your property?

- Will it provide the new buyers with all the conditions that they need for the value that you are selling your property for?

Selling a house is a bit different from buying one, however. Below show the general outline as how to selling your property in a methodically manner: -

Preparation

When deciding how to sell your property, the first thing is to prepare for the sales of the property. Here you must decide on how best to sell your property. You have to consider what options are available, such as: -

- Privately.
- Through an estate agent.
- At Auction.

The factors as to which route we take will be determine on the costs that are involved in selling our property and the level and experience you have in selling property.

Additional cost will be involve in making the property more attractive to the buyer by cleaning and doing necessary repairs, even refurbishing some parts of the property that is outdated to a modern clean look. With all forms of work, you must make sure that the work you are undertaking; firstly that you can do it in a safe environment and have taken all the safety precautions that is needed to do the work properly. If you feel that you cannot do the jobs that are needed, then it is wise to find a local tradesman to do the necessary work for you.

Providing an Energy Performance Certificate (EPC)

You will need to have an EPC ready for potential buyers to see when your property is marketed. You have 28 days to produce an EPC, other wise you are breaking the law. An EPC is valid for 10 years from the date of issue. When you are going to sell your property, one of the first things that you need to do is to have an Energy Performance Certificate sometimes known as an EPC. You will need to provide this to the buyers. An EPC is required by law when a building is built, sold or put up for rent. If you are a landlord or homeowner and need to provide an EPC, you will need to contact an accredited domestic energy assessor. They will carry out the assessment and produce the certificate. Or if you are using an Estate Agent they will want a copy of this in a PDF format. I am not going to say too much about the Energy Performance Certificate here, as I have covered this area in greater detail in the Energy Performance Certificate Chapter.

Selling fees

Depending as to which route of selling your property either via Estate Agents, Online Agent, yourselves or Auctions the choice is totally up to you as to which one you choose as they all have advantages as well as disadvantages. Here you will need to do your homework and choose the one that fits all of your criteria and go along that route. Some of the costs that are involved in how you sell your property can be seen below. This is only a guide as some fees may be higher or lower depending on where you live and the current state of the market.

- Agents normally charge a percentage-based commission usually 1.5% - 4%. This means that the higher the sale price of your home, the more money the Agent will earn.
- With Auction fees it usually amount to 2% of the selling price. Check whether you will be charged separately for

advertising and cataloguing. Keep in mind that you will have to pay the latter even if your house is not sold.

- With Private sale you will usually incur some costs for marketing and advertising. The advantage is that these are one-off costs unrelated to your property's sale price, so clear budgeting is easier.

The Chain

If you are not only selling your home, but also looking to buy a new property, I recommend that you put your house up for sale before you start looking for new properties. This way, you will be able to time the process much better because you will have an idea how quickly you can sell, and you can estimate the possible price range for your new home.

Valuation and Marketing

Once you have prepared your property, the next thing that you need to do is to have the property valued. The property valuator, will value the property based on the size and complexity of the property, and also what other property are been sold for in the same street. Once this part is completed the property now needs to be marketed, so that every one knows that you are selling your property. This can be done depending on which route that you are taking to sell your property through Estate Agents, or Private. If an Estate Agent the marketing will be done for you through their usual channel of advertising and marketing. With private marketing this part you will have do yourself by using the range of resources that are available to you, the local newspaper advertising, websites advertising.

One of the best times for selling property is in the spring and autumn; the market tends to be a bit slower down during late summer and over Christmas and New Year. If a property is sold while the market is buoyant, it's much more likely to attract the asking price.

Negotiation

With any form of negotiation it is always going to be a bit tricky as you will want the highest price paid for your property, and the buyers want the lowest price for your property. This is where negotiations skill can play a big part to determine the final sale price of your property. If you have a set, realistic price for your property keep to and do not go any lower than this, because for every thousand of pounds you lose in sales of your present property is a thousand pound more you will have to find for your new property.

Conveyancing

With regards to conveyancing you have this done for you with your Estate Agent or you can organise this yourself. Decide which methods that suit you best and work in your interests, not the Agents.

PRESENTATION HOME CHECK LISTS

Repairs and maintenance

- Any small jobs that needs doing complete these; that is chipped and cracks, woodwork, replace washers on dripping taps, any painting that need to be done. Any deterioration and outdated paint work do not leave a good impression, but a newly painted doors and gates and any interior or exterior part that needs painting will create a good impression of the property:-

- A well-kept garden, pathway and fence are immediately appealing to potential buyers.
- Check your roof and guttering, and drainage, replacing broken tiles if necessary, clear any drainage blockages as necessary.
- Cutting the lawn can be a last-minute pick-me-up. Feeding it a couple of weeks beforehand will brighten it up and make it look healthy.
- If the kitchen and bathroom units look tired, simply replace, paint or varnish the doors. This will be much cheaper than buying a totally new kitchen or bathroom unit. If the units are in fairly good condition and only look dated, just replace the part that looks dated that is doorknobs, handles and taps.

Look and feel

- Paint walls in a light colour, this will create a good feeling of light and space, enabling buyers to imagine their possessions in the property.
- A blend of good natural light colours that bring out the maximum size of the rooms combine with cushions and accessories to bring out the beauty of the room. Do not use any strong colours, as this will take away all the natural elements the room have to offer.
- Tidy up the rooms as much as possible removing as much of your personal items, such as family photographs and children's drawings, which may distract potential buyers. Buyers want to see them living in the property and can feel at home there, seeing and looking at the property and all owners' possessions can be a hinder. Removing clutter also makes it easier for buyers to imagine their own belongings in a room with their own choice of furniture.

- Flowers and a bowl of fruit will brighten up a room and provide a pleasant smell. The smell of freshly baked bread or fresh coffee though is said to provide a welcoming feel to a home. Plant pots can provide colour in your garden. If you don't have the time to fill your own, you can always get some ready-made.
- With organised rooms, a property will be more appealing. If rooms have a specific purpose this allows buyers to see the full potential of the property. Revitalising a bathroom and kitchen can also be a big positive factor by giving it a fresh clean look. It can make the difference between a sale or not. Buyers want to see light colour suites as coloured suites can have the feel of being old fashioned and may put off potential buyers. So to be safe keep it light and natural as possible.
- If you have pets ask friends or family to look after them during a viewing.
- If you are going to restore for example fireplaces or other period features, think about the cost implications that are involved. Are these changes going to make any difference to the price of your property? It is worth finding out what the maximum likely value for your property will be and the likely returns should you undertake these changes. It is pointless spending £7.000 on restoring or improving features to your property if it will make no difference to the values of your property sales price.

The most important thing is to make viewers feel comfortable. Offer them a cup of coffee and ask them if they need any further information for example, about bills or local amenities.

HOW TO PREPARE YOUR HOME FOR SALE

Selling your home take a lot of preparation get this part right and your property will be sold in no time at all, get this wrong, and your property will not sell like the old saying goes, first impressions really do count.

In order for your property to be sold quickly, you must keep it clean and presentable for viewing. Put yourselves in the buyers' shoes and ask yourselves would you buy this property and being totally honest as to what change I will make if I were to buy this property, Sort out that broken light fixture, the weed-choked garden, giving yourselves a time frame and a budget to prepare your property for sale.

A good starting point is a walk around the exterior of your property with a note pad and pen making notes of all the repairs and maintenance that need to be done. Secondly, go around every single room in the interior of your property making notes of all the necessary work that needs to be done in order to sell your property. Once completed you will probably need to sit down and have a large brandy, contemplating the amount of work you will have to do. This part is the big shock of neglecting the condition of your property. With the remarks as to why did I not do that before. It is too late now to think of that. What we have to do now is to roll up our sleeves and get to work. From now on give yourself a time-frame as to how long it will take you to complete the work load from the exterior and interior on your list of tasks to do. There are some parts that you can do yourselves and there may be some part that is wise to get a professional tradesman to do it for you. Always ensure that before you start any task, that you measure the risks to Health and Safety and your capability of doing the work properly. If you think you cannot do the jobs properly get professional help as it is not worth ending up with a broken leg or other injury if you are not comfortable with for example, height.

You can start either externally or internally this is entirely up to you as how comfortable you feel at this stage, when preparing your property for sale. If you have a front garden and path leading to your front door, invest in a few flowers, place them in a pot or hanging baskets to brighten up the area. This is a good idea when you take your pictures for your advert also attend to the path, clean and clear all the weeds and any stray litter or leaves, also sweep up outside your property. Let your prospective buyers see that your house has been looked after. By running through this short and simple check list and attending to any problems that arise, you have already got past the first step and the biggest. If your property does not look good from the front, people will just drive past and may not even knock on your door. Even worse, if they did ring your doorbell but you could not hear it because you never replaced the batteries when you said you would.

If you do not follow the guide list you are leaving yourself open to a much lower offer than what your property is actually worth. People want to buy your house and move straight in and relax, not arriving with their toolbox to start work immediately, do it all for them, it is well worth going that extra mile.

Exterior appeal

Stand outside your home and compare it to your neighbours' property. By doing this you can have a feeling of what type of work that you need to do. Or better still ask your neighbours or family or friends to give you an overview as to what is needed to improve your chances of selling your property quickly. For any potential buyer to take place we must first impress potential buyers from the outset. Well kept and maintained garden both front and back can do wonders, because from their viewpoint a well maintained outside will reflect a well maintained property in the interior. Most of us have grass in our gardens; this will need to be cut and all the verges need to be trimmed. All dead flower heads need to be removed and thrown away, if you can fork the soil to generate some air and body into the soil, it really does make the flowers stand out.

If you have decking in your garden make sure that it is not damaged in anyway and if possible, give it a fresh coat of paint. Decking is a good selling point in the garden. If you cannot do the work yourselves for whatever reasons get a local handyman to do the work for you. They will be quick and inexpensive and at the same time gives it a very professional appearance in a short time. Purchasers form strong and immediate impressions about how a home looks exteriorly, so make sure yours ticks all the boxes.

- Repaint all exterior woodwork, for example, fill and brush radically to improve the look of the standard three-bedroom family home. Keep lawn tidy and use a pressure washer to clean drives, paths and brick walls.
- Polish all door furniture. It gives the impression of a home that is cared for.
- Be ruthless with the contents of the garage and shed, anything that is not needed get rid of it.

Interior appeal

Homes tend to be covered with photographs of ourselves, friends and family, even that of our pets throughout the property. Take them down and put them in storage and only leave photographs that are neutral and can be seen as pleasant looking features. That is, de-personalise as much as possible so that your buyers can imagine themselves having a lovely life in their potentially new home.

Your buyers do not want to see all the lovely life you have made for yourself in your beautiful home. It gives them an impression that you do not really want to move. They want to imagine their own lovely life they could make for themselves in their beautiful potential new home.

According to research, it usually takes around 20 seconds for a buyer to decide if they like your home after walking into it. Making sure that all entrances are uncluttered, warm and welcoming create a good first impression. Doors should open properly and porches should be cleared of coats, boots and junk.

Hallway

- Place a mirror in the hallway to create an illusory effect of a much larger space.
- Hang a couple of tasteful prints to create interest on a plain wall.

Living room

- Replace any dark, old or dirty carpet with either completely new flooring or new carpet.
- If your floors are carpeted and only mildly stained, hire a carpet cleaner to improve the pile. If you have wooden flooring, give it a polish.
- Throw out old or worn curtains and invest in some brand new ones. There are plenty of quality made-to-measure curtains at affordable prices.
- Use a throw and large scatter cushions to brighten up a tired old sofa.

- De-personalise by clearing out all clutter and family photographs.

Kitchen

- If you are burdened with an inexpensive-looking kitchen but have not got the budget to change it, you can still transform an outdated look with replacement worktops and new cupboard fronts.
- Freshen up tired grout to give tiles an instant facelift.
- Dispose of old fluorescent lighting and replace it with new, modern lighting fittings.

Bathroom

- If you have basic taps and handles, change them for smart-looking chrome or brass fittings to transform the look of the suite.
- Make a feature display of some quality soaps and oils.
- Ensure the bathroom is in clean condition.
- If you have a coloured suite, it is time to replace it with clean, light, space-enhancing white, the preferred choice for homebuyers.

Bedrooms

- Make all beds before buyers visit. Tidy away clothing, personal effects, books etc.
- Reposition furniture to give the effect of maximum space.
- Keep a vase of fresh flowers on the dressing table.
- Open the windows and air each bedroom half an hour before the viewing.

Natural light

Having lots of natural light usually tops the list of things buyers are looking for in a property. It gives that warm and homely feeling. One of the best ways to maximise the light in your house being, natural or otherwise, giving the impression of having plenty of bright and airy space are some simple rules to follow.:-

- Replace dim light bulbs with higher wattage.
- Have light coloured curtains, not dark ones, as this make the room smaller and have a cold feeling at it.
- In areas of your property that are particularly dark, install some extra light fixtures, this can be places like corridors.
- Dark rooms should be repainted with light-coloured and light-reflecting paint.
- Any overgrown trees or vines that are casting shadows inside the property cut these back so that you let in the maximum amount of light in side.

Clutter

We all have clutter from one form or another. That has accumulated over a period of years. A simple rule to follow with all forms of clutter is to get rid of it; this will create more space and make your property more attractive. Also by removing half the furniture in your living room, dinning room, and bedrooms can feel and seam very spacious, sleek and light. With this additional space now available the rooms will feel bigger and there will be lots of space for people to move around without being hindered with furniture thus making the room look smaller.

Here you can hire a skip and get rid of it in one go, or give them to charity. Rent a temporarily storage space unit until your property has been sold. You can store your photographs, furniture, CD, DVDs, Books, Ornaments, etc etc. Homes that are clean and well presented will sell faster than a home with clutters every where. Keep it as a show home in mint condition as this increase the chances of a sale before a buyer has walked through the door. Simple things like tidying up and de-personalising your home will allow the buyer to imagine themselves living in your home. If your furniture is old and outdated, replace it with new or hire it from a specialist company.

Spring clean

This is one of the most important parts to selling a property. If you can remember when you went around the internal part of the property gathering and pin pointing the area that needs to be worked on. This part should have come over and over again in each room. That is clean it. Get this part wrong and it will cost you thousands of pounds, get it right and you can add thousands of pounds to the value of your property. Some points to note here are that you cannot rush these areas. This is a time consuming task, take care to details. It has to be done and done properly otherwise it will look cheap and rushed and may well put off potential buyers.

When it comes to achieving maximum value, it is easy to forget that what is appealing in terms of taste to one person can be less so to another. Of the many home improvement bear in mind the taste of other people when decorating.

- Clean the windows inside and out.
- Dust light fixtures, furniture, cobwebs and skirting board.
- Polish taps and mirrors.
- Replace broken light bulbs.

- Fix leaky taps.
- Fix doors and drawers that don't open or close properly.
- Repair cracks in the walls.
- Paint and repaint where necessary in a neutral colour.
- Hang up fresh towels in the bathroom.
- Get a new shower curtain and bathmat again, choose neutral light shades colour.
- Get rid of out dated wallpaper
- Replace cushion covers, bedspreads and curtains that are worn with new colours and patterns to bring out the best in the room.
- Clean out the refrigerator, cookers, worktops, cupboards.
- Clean out bathrooms and kitchens tiles.
- Vacuum the whole property to get rid of any stain that has accumulated on your carpets. consider having a professional carpet cleaner to clean your carpet.

Pets & other odours

If you have pets it is best to have family or friends to look after them during a viewing. Buyers want to be comfortable during a viewing and do not want to be hindered or frightened of your pets. Another point to bear in mind is that potential buyers do not want the odours of animals when viewing a property as this can be a great put off to some people.

Other odours particularly those from cigarette smoke, mildew can be off putting for buyers. What is needed here is to open the windows and air out the property throughout getting rid of these bad smells. Simply masking bad smells with a perfumed air freshener will not do the trick. With mildew have this removed and get the walls and tile looking clean again.

How to conduct yourself

Presuming that you have elected to show buyers around yourself, how should you go about this? Forget the old advice to bake some bread or put the coffee pot on to make the property smell more homely. Buyers can see straight through such tactics and usually develop a cynical view of your motivations. Whilst the regular smells of domesticity such as cooking or pet dog are certainly not to be recommended, the best scent of all is the background aroma of a good quality air freshener.

The arrival

When your viewers arrive, welcome them and be friendly but do keep things on a professional basis. Over friendliness is a tell-tale sign of someone who is desperate to sell. Your job is to achieve maximum price for your property. Do not show from the outset that you are a soft touch.

Where to start

When beginning the tour, always start downstairs with the best room first and open the door allowing your buyer to enter before you. If you walk into the room before your buyer, the room will appear much smaller to them and could put them off. Avoid obvious statements like: this is the lounge/kitchen etc. People know what room they are in. Allow your buyer to ask questions if they have any but if not, do not be afraid to point out any endearing features or key benefits without going into a long monologue. Keep your facts and selling points short and simple and do not over pressurise them as this can be off putting.

What to look out for

There is a great deal of body language and psychology that go into property viewing. Buyers usually take very little time to look over a property. The average viewing time is only around eight to ten minutes. The longer your buyer takes and the more questions you are asked, the more interested they could be, so try to look at their facial expressions. The more enthusiastic and animated, the more they are interested.

If they ask how quickly you can move or whether the price is negotiable, this is another indication that they have more than a passing interest in making an offer - but it is far from an exact science and you could be asked these questions by people who are not interested in the slightest. If the buyer speaks about the subject of money, always refer them to the agent whose job it is to negotiate on your behalf and achieve the highest price.

If your buyer leaves their name, address or telephone number with you and indicates they may wish to re-visit the property, waste no time in contacting your Estate Agent and telling them. The Agent should carry out a prompt follow-up with the buyer and focus any serious interest towards a re-view as soon as possible.

If your buyer has told you anything about their own position for example, first-time buyer, property on the market or sold etc, ask your Estate Agent to check this information and verify it. Not all buyers are completely honest about their situation and they want to negotiate the price downwards; you only really want to consider this if your buyer is in a good position and you need to sell quickly.

Deciding on an offer

If you have been successful in attracting firm interest from a buyer, the first thing you will receive is a call from the agent putting forward their offer. Usually, this offer will be lower than your asking price although occasionally buyers keen to secure a property or who are fearful of other buyers beating them to it will offer full asking price. The key thing to remember is that the price is not everything in the world of property. Position, too, is important. The Agent checks prior to putting the buyer's offer forward, you should establish how quickly they can move on the offer. Buyers are usually star-rated on their ability to proceed as follows:

Estate Agents

With regards to Estate Agents the question here is, where do we start from as we hear all sort of stories these days about Estate Agents some good and some bad. Finding a good Estate Agent is a tough call, here you have to go with your instinct and trust. If you have any doubts whatsoever avoid getting into a relationship with them as this may create problems later for both of you. This can be a bit worrying as to which one to choose. Whether you are selling a house, flat, cottage, bungalow or apartment it should make no difference to a good Estate Agent to sell. Therefore it is worth looking for Estate Agents that have a good track record of selling similar properties to yours in your area. My advice here would be to do a little bit of research to find a suitable Estate Agent to sell your property; you should contact at least three Estate Agents in your local area. Again ask as many questions to the agent until you are satisfied that they are the one who is best at selling your property. Get this part right and your property will be marketed and sold quickly at the best possible price. Some of the questions that you needs answer to are:-

- A recommendation from a family member or friend can be helpful; a good recommendation can work wonders some times. It may not always mean that their experience and professionalism will reflect upon them doing a good job with your property. But it should be an indication of a good starting point as to what the performance of the estate agent will be.
- Are the Estate Agent properties marketed to a high quality that they are currently selling? Are the pictures of a good quality? Are properties presented as attractively as possible? Are the descriptions accurate? Do you have confidence that the agents will present your property in the best possible light?
- Have they been successful in selling similar properties to yours and do they currently advertise similar properties to yours? If so, they are likely to have lots of buyers on their books already looking for properties like yours. Have a look at the estate agent websites, check to see where they are advertising for example, Rightmove, any other major property websites also, local newspapers. Do they have lots of sales boards as this indicates the strength and presence of the Estate Agent in the local area.

In today's market, it should be a mandatory requirement for any property seller to have their property advertised on the internet with millions of people visiting the big property websites each and every month. If your Estate Agent does not have an internet base, your property will be missing out on a vast numbers of buyers. If they do not have a website base now is the time to change them. In today's world of the internet do not be left behind, get on board and let the agent market your property online as this is the starting point for millions of buyers to look, with nearly 90% of buyers starting their property search on the internet.

Take a look along in any town centre and you are bound to see a host of Estate Agents, each crying out for your business. But which one should you choose? How do you know which one is best suited to sell your home and how do you know you can trust them?

- Test the agent before engaging their services by acting as a prospective purchaser. Make a checklist of how well you are welcomed, how promptly, enthusiastically and professionally are you treated and how thorough the questioning is of your requirements and needs. If you leave with a positive list of all boxes checked, you can be sure if you instruct that agent to sell your home; your buyers will be similarly treated, qualified and handled when introduced to your property.

- A busy Estate Agent office will have lots of activity going on, so watch each office from the street and assess the mood before you walk in. Does the office look well organised and professional looking? Is each negotiator looking busy on the telephone or attending to clients, or are they just leaning back in their chairs looking at their watches, and bored waiting for clients to walk in.

- As a seller, you will want to utilise all marketing opportunities possible to sell your home. Agents offering the longest opening hours should be high on your shopping list of requirements.

- It is no good choosing an agent dealing with the high-end luxury market to sell an average terraced home, and vice versa.

- If the agent has been established for a great many years, it is a sure sign that they have been doing something consistently right over that time. That said, there is nothing wrong in selecting a newly-formed company as it may be staffed with a breadth of experience, but do your research first. It is no good selecting an agent with little experience just because they charge a much lower fee. As in all things, quality often comes at a price.

Your Estate Agents are professional people and they know what to do so, let them show the buyers around. During this time you can go shopping or visit friends until the viewing is completed. By you not being there makes the buyer more relax and does not feel pressurised. Here the prospective buyers can feel comfortable and go through the property picturing what it is like if they where to buy this property. This is the only way that they will get the full impact of the property by wandering on their own.

Since mass use of the internet has come about, there has been an undeniable growth in the number of people selling their homes via alternative means to the conventional high street estate agent. Despite this trend, the vast majority of property sales are still, fortunately, handled by professional estate agents, and indeed the industry itself has made good use of the web as a vital marketing tool.

- They know their market inside out.
- They are aware of the types of properties in an area, the situations of buyers looking for them and the typical values.
- They have their finger on the pulse of local market conditions which may be completely different to the national picture.
- They have an immediate, live register of interested buyers seeking property.
- They know how to pick up and exploit buying signals better than the layperson.

What makes a good agent?

An Estate Agent can be as active or inactive as the market and their need to earn income dictates. However, all good Estate Agents should possess most if not all of the following attributes:Communication skills - letter writing, marketing, selling:-

- Progress chasing - co-coordinating and keeping together complex chains at each of several stages.
- Tenacity - the ability to deal with sometimes difficult solicitors, surveyors and other professionals.
- Peacemaker - placating angry vendors and buyers for whom the agent is always the focus of most blame if things go wrong.
- Diplomacy - sometimes telling people bad news.
- Keeping everything progressing smoothly through to exchange of contracts and ultimately, completion.
- Organisational skills - keeping appointments, making time for clients.

Consumers entering the home-buying or selling process are substantially disadvantaged by the way estate agents currently operate. With over 50% of house sellers who have bought or sold homes say that they have experienced problems with their estate agents services

- Only one in ten buyers and house sellers strongly agrees that estate agents can be trusted.
- Less than a half think that estate agents pass on all offers to house sellers.
- Less than half think that estate agents generally keep home sellers well informed.
- 70% think that estate agents and property developers frequently work together to line each others pockets.

Are they regulated?

Always make sure that the Estate Agents you choose to market your property are regulated and are signed up members of The National Association of Estate Agent, The Guild of Professional Estate Agents or the Ombudsman for Estate Agents. The Property Ombudsman. Members of each organisation voluntarily sign up to a code of practice and are generally taken more seriously than those who are not. All estate agents are bound by the Estate Agents Act 1979, whether or not they are registered with a trade organisation. Selecting an agent who is member of a professional body gives consumers peace of mind. Membership means that the agent must act with probity at all times and that they are bound by strict codes of conduct to which they can be held fully accountable.

All Estate Agents must belong to an approved redress scheme to deal with complaints. Redress schemes will help you if you have a complaint about an Estate Agent.

Fees and costs

Estate Agents will usually charge between 1.5% and 4% of the final sale value of the property as commission. In some cases, you may have to negotiate hard to get an Estate Agent to bring the fee down. Remember, your Estate Agent works on a commission and you want them to be motivated to sell your property fast. Be realistic with negotiations as if you bring the fee down to low, you will take away the incentive the Estate Agent needs to focus on your property sale. Agree a fee that provides a fair deal for both parties. One way could be to pay the full fee if the agent achieves the full asking price and a sliding scale downwards if a lower price is achieved.

There is much more to selling a property than merely taking a photograph, placing an advertisement in the paper and erecting a For Sale board outside the property. The reality is that the physical process of selling a property is relatively easy if the agent has sufficient buyers on their register. The real work of the true, professional Estate Agent begins when a sale has been agreed: keeping all parties informed, progress chasing and managing often tenuous chains.

Contracts

Once you have instructed an Estate agent, you will need to sign a contract detailing an agreement between both of you. This contract set out all of the Terms and Conditions for both parties to follow. This is a legal and binding agreement. Make sure that you read all of the small print in the contract, so you know what you are signing up to. If you have any doubts whatsoever do not signed the contract. Seek legal advice. Any parts that you are not happy with have it amended before you sign. If the Estate Agent refuses to change any parts of it go elsewhere. This is particularly important when thinking about the length of the agreement. You may want to insist on a flexible arrangement, whereby you can review the relationship from month to month. This allows you to switch Estate Agents if your current one is underperforming, otherwise you may have to instruct another Estate Agent simultaneously, with more fees to pay as a result.

Multiple Agents

Multiple Agents is where you instruct one Estate Agent to sell your property, this is called a Sole Agency arrangement. When you agree to a sole agency arrangement with an Estate Agent, the contract will usually indicate how long this period will last. Here you should limit this to a maximum period of three months if possible. At the end of this period you can, if you wish, instruct one or more additional Estate Agents.

If you do instruct one or more additional Estate Agents before the period of sole agency have come to an end, you are breaking the Terms of the Contract with the original Estate Agent and you could be sued. This means that if the new Estate Agent finds a buyer for the house, you have to pay commission not only to the new Estate Agent but also to the agent with whom you had the original sole agency agreement. If the original agent finds a buyer, the amount of commission that the seller would have to pay to the new Estate Agent would depend on the type of agreement you have with them. In some cases, you may be able to negotiate changing the sole agency agreement to a joint sole agency agreement with the original Estate Agent. The strategy of engaging multiple agents is often only for those who are under serious pressure to sell their property fast, as commission fees tend to be higher than with a sole agent.

You may come across some unfamiliar terms in a contract. Make sure you understand what you are agreeing to. The terms sole agency, sole selling rights and ready, willing and able purchaser must be explained in writing if they are used in a contract. Make sure that you understand how much you will have to pay, when and under what circumstances.

Estate Agents Valuation

One of the things that you have to do when you decide to sell your property is to have it value as accurately as possible, in order to determine the potential sale price of your property in the current property marketplace. Property valuations can be a complex and a difficult process. Get the valuation wrong and your property will not sell, or it might sell for less than the property is really worth. A good guide, to start with is seeing

what the properties in your street are selling for, that is of a
similar size to yours. So how should you go about organising a
valuation that accurately reflects the realistic value of your
property? Valuations, however you obtain them, will only ever
be a guide to how much your property might eventually sell for.
Here this will depend on the present market condition and the
demand to property that is similar to yours.

Estate Agents do not routinely conduct a detailed home valuation
of your property, they only indicate, or suggest, an appropriate
Sale Price for the marketing of your Property. Estate Agents
however, are in the best position when deciding on how much
your property can be, or should sell for. It is advisable, however,
to use the professionals to value your property to maximise your
chances of getting the very best price. Some of the larger estate
agents may have experienced valuers working for them, this can
work to your benefit as it will illustrates a truer price of your
property value. They also work to a code created by the Royal
Institution of Chartered Surveyors. This code is based on the
following criteria:

The age and type of property

- The accommodation available.
- The fixtures and features of a property.
- The property's construction and state of repair.
- The position within the locality and the surrounding
  amenities available.
- The tenure, tenancies, services charges or any other
  liabilities.

A detailed property valuation can be different to that of the kind
of valuation your local Estate Agents are able to provide,
because Estate Agents valuation will focus on local trends,

which will incorporate the strength and weakness of the local market, supply and demand of property for Sales or of other similar properties in the local area. The majority of all Estate Agents are providing you with a valuation for free in order to try and win your instruction to sell your property. By having at least three valuation reports from different Estate Agents will also give you an indication as to how much your property is worth, which is why it is recommended you obtain three valuations of your property. Everyone wants to maximise the sale value of their property, but an over-priced property may be difficult to sell, particularly if you are in a hurry to move. This is best from the three valuation of your property you aim somewhere in the middle.

Again as we are in the age of the internet do some searches yourself using one of the large property websites, and search your local area for similar property that are for sale and mostly importantly what price has been paid for properties that have been sold that is similar to yours. By doing this simple research will give you a good indication as to how much your property is worth. If there is a vast difference in price from your own research and that of the Estate Agent, go with you instinct for the price to market your property with. On deciding your valuation, it is important that it is as accurate as possible, buyers will request an independent valuation of a property they wish to purchase, and this will normally be carried out by chartered surveyor. The Surveyor will therefore know if a property has been over-priced or under priced, this may influence their decision to follow through with the purchase or not.

Valuation Methods

There are a number of techniques that are used when assessing the value of a property. These include the Comparable Sales Method, the Income Method and the Cost Approach.

Comparable Sales Method

The Comparable Sales Method is one of the most common methods used in estimating the value of property for sale, this method is based on the prices of similar properties that have been sold in the local area. This method is based upon what the property is likely to sell for.

By using comparable property data that incorporate all relevant market conditions and activity in the area that is collated and characteristics, in such details of recent transactions and features of the property, are analysed. These include:-

- The date of the transactions.
- How the property was paid for.
- How fast the transactions were.
- The property size.
- The condition of the property.
- The location.
- Building regulations, etc.

Once the data has been analysed, an appropriate price range can be set to your property.

The Income Method

The Income Method is different from other methods, because it focuses on the basic value of the property to an individual. This principle is based upon understanding the current market value of the property by assessing the future potential income of the property investment that is its potential re-sale value. An example of this is how much the property value is worth over the next few years. This is normally associated with buy-to-let properties.

The Cost Approach

The Cost Approach looks at the replacement value of the property by understanding the cost of all the relevant components, such as the property itself and the land. The principle here is calculating the value of the land without the building in a free market, establishing the cost of reconstructing the property on the land and then deducting the value of depreciation that has occurred to the building in question.

The most common approaches to property valuations tend to utilise a combination of the Comparable Sales Method and the Income Method.

The valuation price for your property is worth only what a buyer is prepared to pay for it at the end of the day. Here the price will reflect on the area you live and also the demand and supply of such a property you may find buyers are prepared to pay more than the marketed price to secure the property. Similarly, in a weaker market and in a less sought-after area, the opposite is likely to occur. The House Price Index monitors stock levels and asking prices in different regions and the Sold Prices facility offers a simple postcode search of actual selling prices.

Offer agreed

Once the deal has been done and an offer has been agreed, the Estate Agent now has to do certain check on your behalf to verify your buyer's position. Estate Agent will now put both sellers and buyers lawyers in contact with each other to begin the conveyance process and get relevant contracts drawn up. A lot of the work for the conveyance such as searches will need to be done now, but conveyancing can throw up problems down the line which means that the sooner solicitors start talking to each other, the less problematic the process is likely to be.

Selling a property in England & Wales

Finding a solicitor or conveyancer

Many people hire someone who is professionally trained to do the conveyancing, but you could do it yourself. You can use the Law Society searchable datable to help you find a solicitor, in the database you will find contact details for thousands of law firms.

Unless you are a legal expert with strong nerves, you will have to hire a solicitor for the legal and administrative aspects of the sale. Although your expenditure will be lower than when you buy a house, solicitors will still charge you according to the price band your property is in. This can amount to anything between £250 and £500.

Conveyancing can be said to be the process of legally transferring ownership of a property from the seller to the buyer. Conveyancing also includes the various searches and enquiries for example, title search local authority search and any final tasks following the sale. See chapter on Solicitor as this is covered in greater details there. There are three main stages of conveyancing for sellers:-

- Agreement of Sale

- Exchange of contracts
- Completion

Stage 1 - Agreement of Sale

Once the sale of your property has been agreed, you will need to contract a Solicitor or Conveyancer to prepare the legal process and documentations need to be prepared to transfer ownership from you to the purchaser. The sellers are responsible for drawing up a legal contract. If you have hired a solicitor or licensed conveyancer, they will do this work for you. The purchaser will then check the draft contract and may wish to negotiate its contents. The contract contains details including and this can vary for contract to contact:-

- Obtain your title deeds and ask you to fill in a detailed questionnaire.
- Which fixtures and fittings, like carpets and kitchen units, are included in the sale.
- Request a settlement figure for your mortgage and any other secured loans
- How much the property is being sold for.
- Any legal restrictions or rights on the property, like any public footpaths or rules about use of the property, any planning restrictions in place.
- Liaise with all relevant parties and negotiate a date for moving called completion.

Your solicitor or licensed conveyancer will do the following on your behalf:

- Prepare the draft the initial contract and legal information for the contract of sale

- Answer questions from the purchaser's solicitor or licensed conveyancer, they will need your assistance for many of the answers
- Negotiate the details of the contract if necessary

Stage 2 - Exchange of contracts

When both parties are happy with the contents of the contract, the sellers and purchasers will can sign final copies of the contract and send them to each other, so that the exchange of contracts of contact can take place. Once contracts are exchanged, the agreement to sell and purchase the property is legally binding and neither party can pull out without paying some form of compensation at this stage.

Your solicitor or conveyancer will answer any further queries from the buyer's solicitor or licensed conveyancer. The purchaser's solicitor or licensed conveyancer will prepare the legal documents to transfer ownership. You will need to check with the purchasers who will be responsible for insurance of the property once contracts are exchanged.

- Receive the deposit as a down-payment.
- Organise final accounts and prepare a final settlement for your approval.
- Collect any balance of funds required.
- Approve the deed of transfer and arrange for you to sign it.

Stage 3 - Completion

Upon completion of the contract your solicitor will check every thing has been done and completed in regards to the sales of the property both from the buyers and sellers. Then:-

- Pay off the mortgage and notify HM Land Registry.
- Transfer any balance of money to you.
- Transfer of ownership legal documents and deeds are handed over to the purchasers.
- You move out and leave the property in the state agreed in the contract.
- You hand over the keys to the property to the buyer.

"The property now belongs to the new purchasers"

Selling a property in Scotland

In Scotland, sellers usually have an estate agent or developer to market the property for them and a solicitor to process the transaction. In some cases the agent is also the solicitor. I am not going to say a lot about the Scottish system here. I am only going to illustrate just a general guide here and the process that needs to be followed. There are three main stages of conveyancing for sellers:-

- Before an Offer
- Making an Offer
- Concluding an Offer

Before an offer

Before an offer is made, your solicitor will:

- Obtain title deeds from the bank or building society whose loan the house is secured on.
- Request a settlement figure for your mortgage and any other secured loans on your property.
- Receive and process any formal notifications of interest and pass relevant details on to you.

Making an offer

Upon making an offer, your solicitor will:

- Receive formal legal offers from the agent marketing the property, summarise them and ask you what you want to do.
- Confirm with you that the content of any offers is acceptable.
- Recommend changes to offers where necessary and forward alterations to the buyer's solicitor in writing, this process may be repeated a number of times.

Concluding an offer

Upon concluding an offer, your solicitor will

- The seller will have accepted one offer and will instruct their solicitor to complete the missives.
- Once all parties are agreed on the final terms of the offer, including any amendments, a final letter concluding the purchase is sent to the buyer's solicitor.

The solicitor will then:

- Receive full payment for the property on the agreed date of entry from the buyer's solicitor.
- Pass over title deeds and any other relevant paperwork to the buyer's solicitor.
- Repay the mortgage/secured loans (if this apply).

Tax on selling property

If you are selling a property that is your main home you will not have to pay tax on it, provided you satisfy certain conditions. If you are selling a property that is not your main home, it is likely that you will have to pay Capital Gains Tax.

Tax on Sale or Disposal of your Main Home

You do not have to pay tax as long as:

- You bought it, and incurred any expenditure on it, primarily to use it as your home rather than with a view to making a profit on its sale.
- The property was your only home throughout the period you owned it, ignoring the last three years of ownership.
- You did actually use it as your home all the time that you owned it and, throughout that period, you did not use it for any purpose other than as a home for yourself, your family and no more than one lodger.
- The garden and area of grounds sold with it does not exceed 5,000 square meters (about one and a quarter acres) including the site of the house.

If you are married or in a civil partnership and not separated you and your spouse or civil partner can have only one such residence between you. Even if all these conditions are not met, you may still be entitled to tax relief.

Tax on Property that is not your Main Home

You will normally have a chargeable gain if your property is worth more than you paid for it when you sell or dispose of it. However, the first £10,100 of your total taxable gains is tax free (for the tax years 2009-10 and 2010-11).

It is worth bearing in mind that:-

- When working out the chargeable gain you can deduct some of the costs of buying, selling and improving the property.
- If you have made a loss on the property, you may be able to set that off against other chargeable gains you may have.
- If you are living together you can transfer property to your husband, wife or civil partner without having to pay Capital Gains Tax.
- If you give it or sell it cheaply to your children or to others, you may be liable to pay Capital Gains Tax.

HM Revenue & Customs (HMRC) recommends that you keep the following information and documents relating to the property:

- Contracts for the purchase or sale, lease or exchange of the property.
- Any documentation that describes properties you acquired but did not buy yourself: for example, a gift or an inheritance.
- Details of any property you have given away or put into a trust.
- Copies of any valuations taken into account in your calculation of gains or losses.
- Bills, invoices or other evidence of payment records such as bank statements and cheque stubs for costs you claim for the purchase, improvement or sale of the property.

It would also be sensible to keep correspondence with buyers or sellers leading up to the sale of the property.

Capital Gains Tax

Capital Gains Tax is a tax on capital gains. If, when you sell or give away an asset it has increased in value, you may be taxable on the 'gain' (profit). This does not apply when you sell personal belongings worth £6,000 or less or, in most cases, your main home.

Do I have to Pay Capital Gains Tax

You may have to pay Capital Gains Tax if, for example, you:-

- Sell, give away, exchange or otherwise dispose of an asset or part of an asset.
- Receive money from an asset - for example compensation for a damaged asset.

You do not have to pay Capital Gains Tax on:-

- Your car.
- Your main home - provided certain conditions are met.
- ISAs or PEPs.
- UK Government gilts (bonds).
- Personal belongings worth £6,000 or less when you sell them.
- Betting, lottery or pools winnings.
- Money which forms part of your income for Income Tax purposes.

Some points to consider:

- If you are married or in a civil partnership and living together you can transfer assets to your husband, wife or civil partner without having to pay Capital Gains Tax.

- You can't give assets to your children or others or sell assets cheaply without having to consider Capital Gains Tax.
- If you make a loss you may be able to make a claim for that loss and deduct it from other gains, but only if the asset normally attracts Capital Gains Tax - for example you cannot set a loss on selling your car against gains from disposing of other assets.
- If someone dies and leaves their belongings to their beneficiaries, there is no Capital Gains Tax to pay at that time - however if an asset is later disposed of by a beneficiary, any Capital Gains Tax they may have to pay will be based on the difference between the market value at the time of death and the value at the time of disposal.

How Capital Gain Tax is worked out

Capital Gains Tax is worked out for each tax year (which runs from 6 April one year to 5 April the following year). It is charged on the total of your taxable gains, after taking into account:

- Certain costs and relief that can reduce or defer gains.
- Allowable losses you have made on assets to which normally Capital Gains Tax applies.
- The Annual Exempt (tax-free) Amount - this is £10,100 for every individual in the tax years 2009-10 and 2010-11.

Capital Gains Tax Rate

For 2008-09 and 2009-10 Capital Gains Tax is charged at a flat rate of 18 per cent.

The same rate applied for 2010-11 up to 22 June 2010.

From 23 June 2010 the following Capital Gains Tax rates apply:

- 18 per cent and 28 per cent for individuals (the rate used will depend on the amount of their total taxable income and gains).
- 28 per cent for trustees or personal representatives.
- 10 per cent for gains qualifying for Entrepreneurs Relief.

How you pay Capital Gains Tax

You pay Capital Gains Tax through the Self Assessment system. If you have received a Self Assessment Tax Return, follow the guidance to decide if you need to fill in the capital gains pages as part of that return. The return tells you how to obtain these pages if you need them. If you do not usually complete a tax return, but wish to report gains or losses.

Stamp Duty on Property

Stamp Duty is a tax that used to apply to all purchases of property or shares. However when you buy property now you almost always pay Stamp Duty Land Tax (SDLT). Stamp Duty was payable on land and property transactions above a certain value up until December 2003. After 1 December 2003 it was replaced with Stamp Duty Land Tax. Stamp Duty is still payable if you are buying a property where the contract was drawn up before 10 July 2003 and the transfer documents have not yet been stamped. If this applies to you, you can find out more, including how to get documents stamped and the time limits for paying Stamp Duty, in the HM Revenue & Customs (HMRC).

Tax relief when selling your home

Private Residence Relief is the name given to the tax relief designed to ensure that most people do not face a Capital Gains Tax bill when they sell their home.

Who Qualifies for Private Residence Relief?

Generally, if you have lived in your home and it has been your only home all the time that you owned it, you will not have to pay Capital Gains Tax on any money you make when you sell it because it will be covered by Private Residence Relief.

However, you may not qualify for relief on the whole property if you:

- Have a garden or grounds that extend to more than 0.5 hectares (roughly the size of a football pitch).
- Have extensive outbuildings.
- Have used any part of it exclusively for business purposes.
- Bought it primarily in order to make an early sale at a profit.

If you are selling your home and you own more than one property, or you have used part of the property for business purposes, such as using one room as an office, taking in lodgers or letting out all or part of the property for a while, you may be liable to pay Capital Gains Tax.

Whether or not you still qualify for some Private Residence Relief will depend on your exact circumstances, so if in doubt, ask your HM Revenue & Customs (HMRC) Tax Office for advice.

When you no longer live in the property

Even if you no longer live in your property, you can still qualify for the full amount of Private Residence Relief, provided that:

- The property has been your main home from the time that you bought it.
- It has otherwise fully qualified for Private Residence Relief (for example, you have not used part of the property exclusively for business purposes).
- You sell it within three years of moving out or it is no longer being your main home.

Working abroad

If you have been working abroad you will normally be treated as though you have lived in the UK property, and so qualify for Private Residence Relief, provided that both of the following apply to you:

- You live in the property both before and after your absence.
- You have no other home which qualifies for private residence relief.

This relief also applies when it is your husband, wife or civil partner who has been working abroad. You will still get Private Residence Relief for your time abroad, even if you do not return to live in the UK house, provided that the only reason you do not come back to live in your former home is that the employer requires you (or your husband, wife or civil partner) to work elsewhere.

Owning more than one Home

If you live in more than one property you can tell your Tax Office which one you want to be treated as your main home, or principal residence, for Capital Gains Tax purposes. You do have to reside in, not just own, the property to nominate it as your main home.

You have to make the nomination within two years of changing the number of properties you live in, whether the change is an increase in the number of homes or a decrease.

Failing to tell your Tax Office which is your main home

If you do not tell the Tax Office which property you want to call your main home, the question of whether a home that you sell has been your main home and eligible for Private Residence Relief has to be decided on the facts. So it makes sense for you to decide and notify the Tax Office before the two years are up.

You do not have to keep the same house as your main home. Once you have nominated a main home you can tell the Tax Office at any time that a different property should be the one that qualifies for Private Residence Relief but you cannot backdate the change more than two years. You have to reside in a property as your home for it to qualify.

Married couples or civil partners owning more than one home

If you are married or in a civil partnership and have two or more homes, both you and your spouse or civil partner must notify your own Tax Offices which of your homes is your main home for Private Residence Relief purposes - and it has to be the same one. Both of you should sign a notification.

Self-employed and work from home

If you are self-employed and work from home you can still qualify for Private Residence Relief when you sell your home if the whole of your property is used as a home, even though you work there. However, if any part of your property is used exclusively for business purposes, for example as:

- An office.
- A store room.

You may have to pay Capital Gains Tax on part of the gain you make when you sell the property.

Selling a property that you brought for someone else to live in

If you buy a house for someone else to live in and own it but do not live in it yourself, you will not be eligible for private residence relief when you come to sell the property. You are effectively making an investment in a property, so when it is sold at a gain you will be liable to pay Capital Gains Tax on that gain.

One alternative is to give or lend money to the person so that they can buy the property themselves. If the property belongs to them and is their main residence they can claim Private Residence Relief when they sell it.

The law in this area can be complex so consider seeking professional advice. You should also look into the Inheritance Tax implications of making a gift. It is a good idea to ask the

Tax Office for advice when working out what your own position is, as all the factors in your individual situation will need to be taken into account.

If you need to find out more about Capital Gains Tax, contract HMRC. One point to remember is that Private Residence Relief is not available for your property or part of your property if it is used exclusively for a trade or a business.

... And finally...

The best time to sell your property is when the market is strong and demands are high. Therefore, it is advisable that you keep an eye on the property market and time your sale well. Generally, the market tends to be stronger in early and late summer than the rest of the year.

Another point to look out for is low interest rates. Few people are willing to take out a £150,000 mortgage when the Bank of England is raising interest rates. As with inflation running at 4 per cent, the likelihood is that the Bank of England will have to raise interest sooner rather than later to bring down the present inflation level. Also, you should co-ordinate your sale with others in the neighbourhood. If there are already three For Sale signs on your street, it might be better to wait a bit.

In order to time your property sale well, get an overview of the property market by checking what properties similar to yours are selling for. Ask Estate Agents what they are selling and search online property transaction databases for sales in your area.

Up for sale

Experts believe that, if the changes outlined in the consultation document are adopted, many holiday homeowners will choose to sell up in advance of the April 2011 implementation date. If a significant number of holiday homeowners come to the same conclusion, we may see a glut of properties come onto the market in holiday hotspots both in the UK and overseas. The Treasury suggests that there are some 65,000 furnished holiday homes that could fall foul of these proposed changes.

The preferential CGT rate of just 10% on the sale of furnished holiday lets, compared with the usual rates of 18% and 28%, is also likely to play a big part in any decision to sell. There might also be an element of main residence relief in the case of a second home where the necessary tax election has been made, though this is not affected by the proposals.

Depending upon the scale of the business and the timing of the sale, it might be that a sale after 5 April 2011 will still qualify for the 10% tax rate. But the rules are complex and so those looking to hold on to the property beyond that date, but still benefit from this favourable rate should seek proper professional advice. The consultation period ends on 22 October and further information should be available shortly thereafter.

It doesn't matter how much advice you read on the subject of buying and selling properties, it has been and will always be the most stressful thing you will ever do in your life except perhaps getting divorced, dealing with death or getting married! However, if you utilise the full facilities and advice at your disposal from this book you minimise the risks as much as you can and work hard to nurture a relationship with your estate agent, you will dramatically increase your chances of a positive outcome.

Good luck!

5. FREEHOLD AND LEASEHOLD

When we are going to buy or sell our property it is important to know the difference between Freehold and Leasehold property. Most people who own their property already will either know if their property is a Freehold or Leasehold type property. If you are not sure look at the Title documents that you had with reference to the Land Registry. This will state if the property is a Freehold or Leasehold property, or better still request this information from the Land Registry itself. It normally cost about eight pounds.

The terms Freehold and Leasehold refer to the two different ways in which properties in England and Wales can be owned. In Scotland they have their own version of Freehold, called Feuhold. Leasehold Property exists, but it is less common in Scotland than in England and Wales.

It is important to know the differences between freehold and leasehold properties when buying property. Most people will be familiar with the terms freehold and leasehold. Common hold and flying freehold, however, may be new to you, so I am also going to write a little about that. Essentially, freehold and leasehold are types of estates. Commonhold is a new type of freehold. Under the 1993 Housing Act, leaseholders who meet certain conditions have the right to jointly buy the freehold of the entire building, regardless of whether the landlord wishes to sell. The leaseholders can then form their own management company and maintain the building themselves. As an Association this right can only be achieved if all the leaseholders under a freehold wish to buy a share in the freehold, the landlord can still make it very difficult for the leaseholders to do this. The legislation also gives leaseholders first refusal over the Freehold if the landlord wishes to sell.

If you are not familiar with the term Freehold and Leasehold, there are various types of Freehold and Leasehold. I will do by best and explain what they are. Here we go: -

Understanding Freehold and Leasehold

Freehold Property

With regards to Freehold Property this is very simple to understand, and is not as complex as that of Leasehold. This means that when you purchase the Freehold of a property you will own the property, the land on which it was built outright. You may improve the quality and make structural changes to improve the quality of life and modernisation that you like so long as it is within the law, subject to planning restrictions. Any repairs to the property are your responsibility.

One of the few planning restrictions that limit your entitlement in regards to a listed building is that in relation to its structural changes for example. If it is a listed building that has it original single glazed windows, you cannot change these to the lasted double glazed windows.

Freehold properties for sale tend to be that of houses, but there are now an increasing number of Freehold flats that are freehold. With regards to Flat, a share of the Freehold is usually more desirable than leasehold ones, and so is often worth more. This is because of legislation that are now in place is making it easier for Leaseholders to buy the Freehold property.

Flying Freehold

With Flying Freehold this is a bit of a grey area, than a normal standard Freehold property. Flying Freehold is very common like that of as a standard Freehold property. Properties that were built in the 1920's, were built with solid brick of terrace type style houses, which approximately every 6 property has a tunnel type passageway for access to the rear of the property. Above the tunnel passageway, you can see the Flying Freehold part belonging to one of the property, so therefore we cannot consider this type of property to be abnormal from any standard Freeholds property. You should consult a specialist property solicitor if considering buying this type of property. With a specialist property solicitor this process can go through very quickly.

A Flying Freehold is the part of the Freehold property, which overhangs land, which does not form part of that of the main property Freehold. The flying part need not be in mid-air; it can be over a part of someone else's freehold, or over a common part, like a tunnel or passageway between two properties with the upper part has a room in mid-air, or a driveway.

Commonhold Property

Commonhold can be said to be a new system that was introduced in 2004. The majority of properties that are Commonhold are considered to be better than Leasehold and this type of properties are usually to be found in block of flats. Commonhold can be said to be a group of people in a block of Flats who mutually own the Commonhold.

With regards to Commonhold property, a company known as a Commonhold Association owns the Freehold of the building and is responsible for maintaining the communal areas of the building. The owner of each flat is a member of the Association and much agrees to the Terms and Conditions set by the Association. This is similar to that of a lease when you buy a Leasehold property, as there are both advantages as well as disadvantages. The advantages of Commonhold can be said to be that there are no landlords or a set period of time to when you have to leave, as you are one of the Freeholders. The Commonholders Association makes all decisions regarding the building jointly. Commonhold property takes away the concept of a lease and having a landlord. This is the reason why it appeals to buyers. Leaseholders can convert to Commonhold, property, all leaseholders will have to buy the freehold together, this can be a very expensive and difficult process, but you will not lose value, unlike that with leasehold properties. With Leasehold property you will lose the value of the property as the period of the lease gets closer to its expiry date and everyone in the building must agree to convert to Commonhold.

Leasehold Property

If you are to buy a leasehold property, what you are actually buying is the rights to live in a property for a set period of time that is stated in the Lease Agreement until the lease expires. The three mains cost that is associated with a Leasehold property is the: -

- Actual Purchase Cost. The Price paid for the property.
- Ground Rent. This is in most case an annual rent is a levy on the building for occupying the owner's land.
- Maintenance Cost. This is generally a service charge to cover the maintenance of the building.

As a leaseholder, you are in no way obligated to retain the lease. You can sell up at any time. Once the set period in the lease expires, the ownership of the property is given back to the freeholder or owner. Most leases have a life span of roughly 99 years; however. It is possible to extend the leasehold to up to 999 years, with an option purchase the freehold, but at a cost if you buying a Leasehold property, it is very important to find out how long the lease has left, as this will affect the value of the property. Be also careful as that the lease has under fifty years left as some Banks and Mortgage Company will not give you a mortgage.

Most Banks and mortgage lenders do not have a problem with providing you with the loan to buy a leasehold property, as long as the lease is long enough. . They usually have a limit of around 50 years on the terms of a lease. With property under 50 years, check first with the banks to see if they will lend you the money for the property. This is changing slowly thanks to new legislation that has been coming now. This makes it slightly easier to purchase the freehold or extend the lease of property now.

You will not actually own the property, or the grounds it is situated on. The majority of properties that are leasehold are flats, though some house can be leasehold to. With leasehold property, you are obligated to pay ground rent to the freeholder or landlord. The ground rent or Service Charge will cover the costs for communal maintenance repairs of the building for e.g. external redecoration and repairs, insurance, gardening, window cleaning; buildings the normal fees here will be stipulated in the lease agreement.

The cost of leasehold properties can be cheaper to maintain than that of freehold properties, because most flats are leasehold, and this means everyone living with in the same building has to share the maintenance costs in respect of the common parts of the building and the communal areas. One of the main advantages is that it has clear responsibilities for the upkeep and repairs, at the same time protecting the individual leaseholder, in the event of, for example, a leak from the flat above. Unlike a freeholder where the total cost is met by the person who owns the freehold.

The Lease

The lease is a legally binding document detailing the rights and responsibilities of the freeholder and leaseholder. The lease has clear Terms and Conditions set out for which the property is occupied and used. These conditions are imposed to protect all interested parties, including the freeholder and any other tenants.

Leaseholders are usually entitled to quiet enjoyment of their property. This responsibilities include paying the relevant charges on time, keeping the inside of the property in good conditions and order, conducting themselves in a neighbourly fashion, and not doing some things for example, sub-letting the property or running a business from it, or making certain alterations without the freeholder's permission.

The freeholder also has responsibilities include maintaining the common parts of the building, ensuring that each leaseholder complies with the Terms and Conditions of the lease.

When considering the purchase of a leasehold property, always make sure that you understand what the Terms and Conditions are and what the lease entitles you to do. If you are unsure, please seek legal advice form a property solicitor who has experienced with dealing with lease properties. Do not sign a Lease Agreement until you are one hundred percent sure that you know every thing that you need to know about the lease of the property that you are purchasing.

When you are buying a leasehold property, ask your solicitor to make sure that the previous leaseholder is up to date with all payments for e.g. ground rent and maintenance payments. In some cases any arrears occurred are carried with the property not the leaseholder, this mean that you become liable for payments form the previous occupants that they have failed to make.

Even though Landlords and Managing Agents still have some power over leaseholders, recent Government interventions have been redressing the balance of power to some degree and slowly reforming a system that has at times been abused by the Landlords and Managing Agents. In the 1996 Housing Act, the leaseholders have the right to take their landlords to a Leasehold Valuation Tribunal (LVT), if they are unhappy with the level of service they are getting for the cost of the service charges. The cost of taking a landlord or freeholder to an LVT whose decision is legally binding, you may have to pay up to £500 to appeal. The actual amount depends on the reason for your application and if you are asked to attend a hearing, no matter how many leaseholders are involved.

As a result, you can no longer be served notice for refusing to pay high maintenance costs unless these have been ruled as fair by the LVT. The LVT is an independent legal body that offers a fair way of settling a dispute without the need to go to court. Their decision is legally binding and they can deal with disputes about, service, administration or management charges, appointing a manager for a block of flats, building insurance, buying the freehold, varying or extending a lease. Landlords can also ask the LVT for permission not to consult leaseholders about service charges. This is known as 'dispensation with service charge consultation.'

Terms and Conditions

If you break the Terms and Conditions of your lease, you may lose your property or you may have to compensate the freeholder. The freeholder must give you written notice and a set time to make the right the wrong. This is also the same process of the leaseholder if the freeholder breaks the Terms and Conditions of the Lease Agreement, for example, by failing to maintain the common parts adequately or imposing a very high maintenance charges that cannot be justifiable.

Leasehold Management

Leasehold properties can be managed in a numbers of different ways. For example, the Freeholder or residents' management committee deals directly with management issues. In others, an agent is appointed to handle the managerial side for a fee. This can be either a Fixed Charge or a percentage service charges payable by each leaseholder paying a share. Since the introduction of the right to manage, leaseholders may be entitled to manage the building as if they were the freeholders even if they do not own the freehold.

6. MORTGAGES

With hundreds of mortgage deals that are on the market, it is hard to know where to start from. One of the best ways is to use a mortgage broker, or shop around, or go direct to the lender. Whatever method that you have decide upon, it is important to understand how mortgages are regulated and sold. If you are thinking about taking out a mortgage you should make sure you look into all the different options available to you, and that you only borrow what you can afford to pay back. If you do not keep up the agreed repayments, the lender can take possession of the property.

A mortgage is a loan you take out to buy your property. Most banks and building societies offer mortgages, as well as specialist mortgage lenders. If you change lenders but do not move home it is referred to as a re-mortgage. The Financial Services Authority (FSA) regulates the way most mortgages are sold, but not second-charge and most buy-to-let mortgages. This means firms must follow certain rules and standards when dealing with you.

If you wish to buy a property you may be able to borrow money to do this. This is called a mortgage. The loan is for a fixed period, called a Term and you have to pay interest on the loan. If you do not keep up the agreed repayments, the lender can take possession of the property. If you are using a mortgage to buy your property, you will need a need a formal mortgage offer from your lender before you sign the contract to purchase your property. The lender will send documents for you or your solicitor or conveyancer to sign.

For some groups of people, such as first-time buyers and key workers, it may also be possible to borrow some of the money you need to buy your property from other government-backed sources. You will usually need to borrow the rest of the money from a normal mortgage lender such as a bank or building society. As well as standard mortgage deals, lenders might also offer deals which are especially designed for people who do not qualify for a standard mortgage. This type of deal is known as a sub prime or adverse credit mortgage. These are aimed at people who have had financial difficulties or credit problems in the past. For example, you might have had a previous home repossessed, have a County Court Judgment (CCJ) against you, or have been declared bankrupt by the Courts. Also some self-employed people may also have difficulty in proving a regular or reliable source of income.

Sub prime and adverse credit mortgages usually charge a higher rate of interest than standard mortgages. Lenders may also limit the amount of money they are prepared to lend you. Before taking out a sub prime or adverse credit mortgage, you should get some independent financial advice.

Where to get a mortgage from

A mortgage could be available from a number of different sources. Some of the available options are:-

- Building societies.
- Banks.
- Insurance companies.
- large building companies might arrange mortgages on their own new-build homes.
- Finance houses.
- Specialised mortgage companies.
- Mortgage Brokers.

Mortgage application process

Once you know roughly how much you want to borrow and have identified your preferred lender, there are some key stages to follow to get a mortgage. These are the same whether you are borrowing for the first time or changing lender for e.g. re-mortgaging your property.

When you choose a mortgage, you will need to think about how you are going to repay the mortgage and which are the best method that is available to you, for example, interest rate deals and special features of some mortgages. The best one for you will depend on your circumstances, so it is important to understand your options and shop around for the best deals that are available to you.

You can get a mortgage direct from the lender, banks, building societies and specialist mortgage lenders, or you can use a mortgage broker. With the growing use of the internet now, mortgages are now available online, all you have to do is fill out your mortgage form online following the instruction that is given to you, if you are computer literate and know your way around a computer this methods is possibly your best option, otherwise get the Banks or Mortgage Broker to fill it out for you. There are several types of mortgage available. The two main ways to repay your mortgage are repayment and interest only.

With a repayment mortgage you make monthly repayments for an agreed period until you've paid back the loan and the interest.

With an interest only mortgage you make monthly repayments for an agreed period but these will only cover the interest on your loan endowment mortgages work in this way. You will normally also have to pay into another savings or investment plan that will hopefully pay off the loan at the end of the term.

The most common ones are described below:-

Repayment mortgage

This is a mortgage in which the capital borrowed is repaid gradually over the period of the loan. The capital is paid in monthly installments together with an amount of interest. The amount of capital which is repaid gradually increases over the years while the amount of interest goes down. With a repayment mortgage you make monthly repayments for an agreed period until you have paid back the loan and the interest assuming you can afford it, the safest way ahead would be to take a repayment mortgage in which you steadily pay off both the interest and a small chunk of the loan each month.

Flexible features

Some mortgages offer you options to vary your monthly payments, or to combine your mortgage account with savings and other income, these are called flexible, current account and offset mortgages.

Interest only mortgage

With an interest only mortgage you make monthly repayments for an agreed period but this will only cover the interest on your loan. You will normally also have to pay into another savings or investment plan that will hopefully pay off the loan at the end of the term. With this type of mortgage, you pay interest on the loan in monthly installments to the lender. Instead of repaying the loan each month, you pay into a long-term investment or savings plan which should grow enough to clear the loan at the end of the mortgage term. However, if it does not grow as planned, you will have a shortfall and you will need to think about ways of making this up. Any shortfall after the term of the mortgage term will have to be met from you in some way to cover the short fall. For lower percentage borrowers, lenders might offer you the choice of an interest-only loan. This will be easier on your cash flow and has been favoured by many buyers in the past but is also a riskier choice.

You will also find a range of interest rates to choose from, for example, variable and tracker rates change in line with Bank of England rates, fixed rates are fixed for a set number of years, whereas capped rates have a variable interest rate with a ceiling so your payments will not go above a set amount.

There are three main types of interest-only mortgages. These are:-

- **An endowment mortgage**. This mortgage is made up of two parts, the loan from the lender and an endowment policy taken out with an insurance company. You pay interest on the loan in monthly installments to the lender but do not actually pay off any of the loan. The endowment policy is paid monthly to an insurance company. At the end of the mortgage term, the policy matures and produces a lump sum which should pay off the loan to the lender. In some circumstances, an endowment policy may produce an additional lump sum. However, there is also a risk that it will not be worth enough to pay off the loan at the end of the mortgage term. If you have been told by your endowment provider that your policy will not be enough to pay off your loan, you should seek independent financial advice.
- **A pension mortgage**. This mortgage is mainly for self-employed people. The monthly payments are made up of interest payments on the loan and contributions to a

pension scheme. When the borrower retires, there is a lump sum to pay off the loan and a pension.
- **An ISA mortgage**. With an ISA mortgage, you pay interest to the lender, and contributions to an Individual Savings Account (ISA) which should pay off the loan.

Self-certification mortgages

If you can not prove your income perhaps because you are self-employed and do not have accounts going back far enough, you may be able to get a self-certification mortgage. Although you may not have to offer proof of income to the lender, the lender will still want to be sure that you can afford the repayments so may ask you to provide evidence of your other outgoing.

For those who are self-employed or have a fluctuate level of income, lenders may want to see more documentation of evidence of income proof. Apart from the last two years accounts and possibly the last 12 months bank statements, lenders have also been asking for form SA302, which shows the tax calculation made by the Revenue. This is something that many do not necessarily receive as a matter of course and it will need to be specially requested, slowing down an application. The frustrating part is that there seems to be no uniformity to what lenders will ask for and when. Decent independent mortgage brokers will know which lenders are moving quicker than others and what they are likely to ask for at any given time.

<u>Interest rate deals</u>

As well as deciding on your repayment method, you will need to look at the interest rate deals on offer. Suitability of different deals will depend on your personal circumstances and any tie-ins or penalties that may be attached. Below are some of the common interest rates are available, for example:-

Standard variable rate

With a variable rate mortgage your payments go up or down with the lender's standard interest rate. This often changes following Bank of England base rate changes.

Standard variable rate with cash back

With these deals you get a cash lump sum as well as the loan when you take out the mortgage. You're usually tied into the variable rate for a set period.

Discounted rate

You pay a lower interest rate to begin with then move to another rate usually the lender's standard variable rate after a set period.

Tracker

Tracker rates are linked to the Bank of England rate or some other base rate. This means they will always go up or down in line with changes to the base rate.

Fixed rate

You pay a fixed rate of interest for a set period, so you know exactly what you will be paying each month during that time. When the fixed period ends, you will usually move to the lender's standard variable rate. There are usually penalties if you pull out early.

Capped rate

With a capped rate you pay a variable interest rate, there is an upper limit so that your payment will not go above a certain amount for a set period. This is the lowest rate you will get. If interest rates fall below the capped rate, you will lose out.

Flexible, current account and offset Mortgages

Flexible, current account and offset mortgages give you more control to vary your monthly payments. They can be used with repayment or interest only mortgages. For example you can:-

- Pay less one month and more the next.
- Make lump sum repayments and sometimes draw these back.
- Take a payment holiday.
- Pay off your mortgage early.

How lenders decide how much you can borrow

When you take out a mortgage, lenders look at a number of things to work out how much you can borrow. These include your earnings and outgoings, the property value and your credit history. Whatever you borrow, you need to be sure you can afford the repayments.

Your earnings

Lenders have in the past offered to lend money based on the level on earnings. Recently it has become more common for lenders to make an affordability assessment when calculating how much they will lend you. In terms of documentation, lenders will want to see your last three months' payslips and last P60 as well as potentially your last three months' bank statements.

Borrowers need much more paperwork these days to verify their income and ability to repay these must be sequential with no single statement missing. Be warned that many lenders do not like internet bank statements, even though they encourage their own customers to switch to online statements. If purchasing, proof of the deposit monies will also be required. If this is a lump sum that has suddenly appeared in your account then they will want to know the origins of this.

It is important to give your lender as much details and information as possible about your earnings and outgoings so that you are offered a mortgage that you can afford to pay back, and are suitable to you.

Credit History

Your lender will check your credit history and ask previous lenders or landlords for references. If your record shows that you have had difficulty with loans or rent payments in the past, it may affect how much you can borrow. Do not be put off if a lender refuses you a mortgage or offers you an expensive deal, it is still worth shopping around. Your lender may get written references from your employer and bank or accountant if you are self-employed and from your current lender or landlord. They will also run credit checks to make sure you have paid off your debts in the past.

The first stage to overcome is the lender's credit score. A good three-year address history is a must and it helps dramatically to be registered on the voter's registry at your current address. The amount you can borrow is no longer simply linked to a multiple of your income, but on an affordability basis linked to the credit score.

Monthly outgoings are taken into account, so a small credit card you could pay off, but choose just to pay the minimum, will affect your borrowing. The number of dependents you have also has a bearing on the loan, as will any outgoings such as childcare. This means that although you are on the same incomes as, a couple with no children or credit card debts, they may be able to borrow substantially more than you with one or more children and outstanding credit card balance.

There are many good borrowers who are being turned away every day for reasons they cannot quite work out. The days of simply chasing the cheapest rate, armed with a passport and a smile, are long gone. As with most things in life, cheapest does not necessarily mean the best. The lender may not lend you the required amount in the timescale needed at all. Of course, it is not necessarily a bad thing that lenders have become more prudent. But there are many good borrowers who are being turned away every day for reasons they cannot quite understand.

Using a broker to get a mortgage

Instead of going directly to a lender such as a building society for a mortgage, a broker could be used. A broker may be an estate agent, or a mortgage or insurance broker. They will act as an agent to introduce people to a source of mortgage loan to help them buy a home.

You may want to use a broker because it can save you time shopping around. However, some lenders offer products direct to customers which a broker may not be in a position to offer. So, it may be best to shop around to see what else is available. There are rules about how much a broker can charge for their services. Also, brokers must not discriminate against you because of things like your disability, race, religion or belief, sex or sexuality when they are offering you their services.
Mortgage brokers must be authorised by the Financial Services Authority (FSA) or must be agents for authorised firms. The

FSA is the UK's financial regulator set up by government to regulate financial services and protect your rights. Its standards require firms to be competent, financially sound and to treat their customers fairly.

This means mortgage firms have to give you certain documents with the keyfacts sign. Keyfacts documents are set out in a standard format to help you compare different services and products with each other. The two mortgage keyfacts documents are: Keyfacts about our mortgage services and Keyfacts about this mortgage.

Check that your adviser is authorised

Provided you deal with an FSA-authorised firm or the agent of an authorised firm, you will have access to complaints and compensation arrangements. To check whether a firm is authorised you can use the FSA's register service.

Making a complaint about a mortgage lender

If you want to complain about a mortgage lender or broker, you should first discuss the problem with them, and then consider making a formal complaint. If you think the mortgage lender or broker has discriminated against you, you can complain about this as well. Each lender or broker should have its own internal complaints procedure. If you have followed this procedure and are still not satisfied, you can take your complaint to the Financial Ombudsman Service.

Agreement in principle

A lender or mortgage adviser may offer to give you an approval or agreement in principle. This set out what the provider will probably be willing to lend you based on certain terms and conditions. This can be helpful when you have chosen your mortgage and are ready to make an offer on a property. Never be tempted to overstate your income. You could end up with a mortgage you can not afford.

Solicitor or licensed conveyancer

Instead of using a broker or financial adviser, you can shop around and arrange a mortgage directly with a building society, bank or specialist mortgage company. A useful starting point might be to compare what is on offer on the FSA's impartial mortgage tables. Of course lenders will only recommend from their own mortgage range, but may have several you can choose from. You will still receive the Keyfacts documents described above.

Mortgage application

When you have decided to buy a property, you make a full mortgage application by completing and returning the lender's form you can sometimes do this over the phone. They will usually also want to see evidence of your income, your identity, your current address and, where relevant a previous lender or landlord's reference. They may also want a non-refundable fee to cover their costs and perhaps to pay for a valuation. If you cannot prove you have got a regular income maybe because you are self-employed and do not have enough proof you may be able to get a self-certification mortgage. This usually requires a larger deposit and the lender may still want some evidence of your ability to pay.

Property valuation

Your lender will usually have the property valued to make sure it is worth the price you have agreed to pay. If it is not, it could affect how much they will lend you. It is advisable to get your own survey done too or to upgrade the lender's valuation survey to a more detailed one. Your lender will arrange a valuation to check how much the property's worth.

The mortgage offer

If the lender is happy with the valuation and references, you will be made a formal offer, usually sent to you and your solicitor. Once you or your solicitor on your behalf have signed and returned the offer documents, your lender is committed to providing the money. The mortgage offer usually requires you to take out buildings insurance, in case something happens to the property before you have paid off the mortgage.

Exchange and completion

If you are buying, once you have got a formal mortgage offer, your solicitor can agree a date for exchanging contracts with the seller's solicitor. At this time you usually pay a percentage of the purchase price as a non-refundable deposit and commit to paying the rest on the agreed completion date when the property becomes yours.

Insurance

A lender may require you to take out life insurance to pay off your mortgage should you die, known as Mortgage Protection Life cover. You can also get insurance to protect your income or just your mortgage payments if you become ill or disabled, or lose your job, known as Mortgage Payment Protection Insurance (MPPI).

You will also need to take out Building Insurance for the property, with the Mortgage Lender as the Interested Party as they have a vested interest in the property. The Insurance Schedule will have your name and the interested parties name as well together with as to how is covered and the level of excess you have to pay if you make a claim. With all forms of insurance it is essential that you maintain a fully comprehensive policy at all time. This way you are always covered if something goes wrong. I will always say that with building cover it covers the total cost of rebuilding your property should it be damaged by an insured incident. Always have full rebuilding cost insurance. If you are not clear as to what is covered contact the insurance company and get them to explain to you as to what is covered.

The Disadvantage of obtaining a mortgage

Obtaining a mortgage is no longer as easy as it was a few years ago, as we have house prices falling, banks are not lending unless you have a high deposit. In recent weeks there has been a lot of talk about a decline in the levels of lending for mortgage purposes by both banks and building societies.

The British Bankers' Association (BBA) suggested that the main cause of this was a lack of consumer demand. Lenders suggest they are providing almost all their applicants with the mortgages they apply for directly. But there are many tales of woe from seemingly decent borrowers who have either been turned down or, more commonly, been told that they can only borrow a lot less than they need.

Difficult for borrowers

The difficulties some face in obtaining mortgage finance is all the more frustrating because the numbers of overall mortgage products have increased. There are now some excellent choices, whatever your individual views on interest rates are. Trackers under 2%, five-year fixes below 3.7% and deals that allow you to enjoy a low tracker now and to switch to a fix without penalty at any time are on offer. Many of these products come with a free valuation and legal fees paid for re-mortgages.

Whilst this all sounds great, the reality is that most of these products are only available in the low loan-to-value, (LTV) arena, around 70% and below. In order to really help the country as a whole however, there has to be more innovation in the 80% to 90% loan-to-value market. Lenders, who currently operate in this area, seem to make it very difficult for many borrowers to actually obtain the offer they request.

For those looking at borrowing, getting your documentation right and preparing before you start applying for a mortgage is the key to success. The amount you can borrow is no longer simply linked to a multiple of your income.

7. ESTATE AGENTS, ONLINE OR PRIVATE

Estate Agents Services

When we are selling or buying a property we normally go to an Estate Agent to market our property for us, this is known as the tradition or grassroots type of marketing. But in today's world of the internet there are other ways to market your property, we now have online Agents, or we can market the property ourselves. We are typically spoilt for choice now. I will try to explain the various ways to buy or sell your property, whichever methods you choose there will always be pros and cons. That is the main reason to take your time and work out the best ways that suit you. Estate Agents can perform the whole selling and buying process you. If, however, you do not just want to sit back and let the Estate Agent do everything for you, you should make this clear from the start that you want to be involved. In order to maintain a good working relationship with your Estate Agent, it is important that you decide on how much you want to participate, and let the agent know about it before you start the process of buying and selling your property.

Estate Agents in the United Kingdom can be said to be, a business that arranges the selling, renting or management of homes, land and other buildings. However in many instances, Estate Agents are mainly engaged in the marketing of property available for Sale and a solicitor is used to prepare and exchange contracts. In Scotland, many solicitors also act as estate agents, a practice that is rare in England and Wales.

Regulation

At the present time there is no legal requirement to belong to either organisation in order to trade as an Estate Agent. Some Estate Agents are members of the Royal Institution of Chartered Surveyors, (RICS), the principal body for UK real estate professionals. However, the vast majority of RICS members known as Chartered Surveyors who practice in Estate Agency do so with commercial properties. For residential property a Trade Association known as, The National Association of Estate Agents (NAEA), exists, but as a non-professional body it has limited scope for disciplining members when appropriate Due to the lack of effective regulation, dishonest and fraudulent practices may exist in the industry. It would be foolish to use an agent who is not a member of a trade body or ombudsman scheme, so check with the National Association of Estate Agents (NAEA) or the Ombudsman for Estate Agents (OEA) for members in your area.

Estate Agents have a mixed reputation and some have fallen into disrepute lately, as a result of unfavorable news coverage. However, over 90% of properties are still sold via an Estate Agent. It is true that, apart from the OFT, there is no independent body regulating all Estate Agents, and that Agents do not need any qualifications to practice their profession. The Property Ombudsman has introduced a complaints procedure, which should cover most agents, and it is also possible to complain to The Office of Fair Trading. The Ombudsman for Estate Agents Scheme, which obtained the British Government's Office of Fair Trading (OFT) approval for the Code of Practice for Residential Sales in 2005 and, as of November 2006, it has about 2500 member agencies. The Department of Trade and Industry (DTI) recently proposed that all Estate Agents join an ombudsman service. Many have already done so, and thousands of complaints are investigated each year. Even the National Association of Estate Agents wants more regulation in the industry. It offers a wide range of training courses, but only the most reputable firms insist on these qualifications for their staff. All Estate Agents are required to register with an Estate Agents Redress Scheme that has been approved by the Office of Fair Trading (OFT) and which investigates complaints against estate agents. The Property Ombudsman is one of the schemes approved by OFT.

If you have a Complaint

Estate Agents have their own Ombudsman who mediates between member estate agents and their customers in the event of a dispute. The advantage of choosing an estate agent who is registered with the Ombudsman is that if you have a complaint about your estate agent, this can be easily be resolved through the Estate Agent own complaints procedure, the Ombudsman can act on your behalf if they think you have a valid complaint.

The advantage of using an Estate Agent is that they have all the tools for the job to help you sell or buy a property that is they have an office, they advertise your property in the local newspaper, use also online marketing, they will help you with any advise you may need, arrange buyers and sellers for your property, etc., hope you get the picture as to what I am analysing here.

The importance of the Estate Agents Fees

An Estate Agent selling a residential property generally charges between 1.5% to 4% of the sales price plus VAT as commission. Do not forget that you will be charged VAT of 20 per cent of the Estate Agent's commission, but their fees are negotiable if you push them a bit as the market is very competitive. What is more, because Estate Agents need you more than you need them, you are going to be pleasantly surprised at how effective your negotiation skills will be on the estate agents fees for selling a house. You may find that the National Estate Agents are more difficult to negotiate than the smaller independent estate agents. The National Estate Agencies tend to operate and impose stricter policy regarding their commission levels, and sales target for their staff. The advantage of a smaller independent estate agent is that they tend to work a lot harder to sell your property than the larger Estate Agent. You also have the personal touch together with negotiable a better deal with regards to Agents fees. The coverage can be just as good as any National Estate Agents because they all have much the same style as advertising, that within the Estate Agents, newspaper, online.

Estate Agents will also be higher in cities and town comparison to the rural part of the UK because rent and salaries and other overhead cost are much lower, for example, selling a property in London compared to that of Birmingham. One of the most important thing to remember is that you are in the driving seat and all these Estate Agents want your business, so choose carefully and satisfy yourself that you are happy with the Estate Agent that you have chosen in terms of service provided, costs, how quick that properties are selling. Point to remember is that if an estate Agent is busy, it may not mean that they are also the best, it may mean that they are busy at only the enquire level only and not actually selling any property like other Estate Agents.

This will also depends on the contractual arrangement you have and whether an individual firm has sole rights to the sale. If the Estate Agent is the Sole Agency, which means they have the exclusive right to sell your home for about eight to twelve weeks, the commission paid will be lower than if you have a joint sole agency. You could instruct two Agents to work together on your behalf and share the commission or have a multiple agency agreement. A multiple Agency agreement is where you have a number different Estate Agents compete to sell your house and do not share the agreed commission.
With any forms of contract always read the small print and make sure that you understand the Terms and Conditions on the

Contract before you sign. If you have any doubt whatsoever do not sign any contract, ask for clarification of the contract and make sure the level and quality of advertising is sufficient for your needs. An Estate Agent's commission is usually based on whether there is one or more Estate Agency instructed for the Sale of the property.

Estate Agents Services

Suggest an Asking Price

One of the first thing an Estate Agent will do is to suggest an asking price for your property, if their suggestion value is to low, tell them your own idea as to how much you think your property is worth. Look to see how much the property value in your street is selling for. Others factors to take into consideration when you are selling your property is how quick you need your property to be sold, this will reflect on setting the asking price of your property, the present condition on the housing market. Before choosing an Estate Agent you should compare your local Estate Agents with other Estate Agents online property advertising, selling performance and average property price by looking them up in the in various search engine site that are available online for example, Zoolpa, Estate Agent Directory, Rightmove.

Presentation and Advertising

One of the most important roles of an Estate Agent is in the form of Presentation and Advertising of your property. Here the Agent comes to your property to see the condition and state of the property. The Agents will compile a detailed description of your property, measure the size of the property taking into account the feature of the property such as fire place, type of heating system, they will take pictures of your property for presentation and advertising. Before the presentation and advertising begin check to see that you are happy with the presentation materials and property description before they are listed with the agents in various coverage that the Agents uses to advertise their property. This can be difficult to change afterward.

Estate Agents may vary their form of advertisements from that of other Agent to have a better competitive edge, but most Estate Agents will list your property in their windows and brochures. Some also place ads in property magazines or local papers, while most have a website with property listings. A good Estate Agent will make sure that the advert reaches the target audience with flyers in certain area for certain type of property. As most buyers now start their search for a home online it is more important than ever to ensure that your chosen estate agent advertises widely on the web.

Viewings

With regards to arranging the viewing of your property, this can be done either by the Estate Agent or yourselves. If you let the Estate Agent to arrange and perform the viewing you make incur additional charges. You may wish to show potential buyers around your property yourself in order to point out all its advantages your property has. You may make a better salesperson that the agent because you know the property a lot better. Most Estate Agents are fairly flexible when it comes to this arrangement.

Prepare to Negotiate

Take every effort possible to make your property look its best both inside and outside for the Estate Agents valuation appointment, as this will determine the price of your property. I generally recommend that you have a fairly good idea of how much your property is worth, and how much you are prepared to sell it for. It is better to start with a high but realistic value in which you can negotiate down at a later stage if the property does not sell within your time frame. Well-presented houses are easier to sell. When Estate Agents see a well presented property they are more motivated to secure you as a client. A realistically priced property is a lot easier to sell a lot quicker than an unrealistic price property which can be difficult to sell. No clients will be interested in your property.

Estate Agents are professionals in negotiation. Do not lose sight of the fact that Estate Agents are salesmen, stand your ground and be firm. Simply tell the Estate Agent that, if they can not match their competitor's rate, you will have no choice but to give your business to their rival agent. The ball is now in the agent's court and if they want your business they will be forced to make you their best offer. It is now up to you to decide if it is tempting enough for you to employ them.

As a golden rule always let the agent know you still have other agents to interview and that you will be in touch to inform them of which agent you have chosen in due course. Make a note of each Agent Fees to the service that they will offer. If the agent you like the best is not the one with the lowest fee, you should then try the following strategy, ring the agent again stating that you are torn between his agent and another agent. Explain that you feel both agents would provide the level of service you require from an agent and that you are sure either one is capable of finding you a buyer. But the one with the lowest fee-levels will be the deciding factor over whom you choose to do business with. The reason I have mention the above is that we must treat estate agents like any form of business. They need our service more than we need theirs, so negotiate the best price you can possible get without lowing the standard of work that is to be achieved.

Valuations

Some agents inflate the valuations to get the houses onto their books. Once they sign up the vendors, they gradually encourage them to drop the price to get a sale. Honest agents miss out on business because their realistic valuations are rejected by greedy homeowners. Valuations are among the most common complaints about estate agents. Research by Which Magazine, as part of the Move It campaign for the regulation of estate agents, found that valuations could vary by as much as 63%. But some less scrupulous agents have been accused of putting off prospective buyers and pushing lower offers from property developers in return for a slice of the profits.

Another marketing ploy that infuriates local residents is the fly boarding of properties that are not for sale, consumers can be fooled into thinking an agent is the hottest in the area because of the high numbers of their For Sale boards that they can see. Undervaluation can also work to an agent's advantage. This is particularly the case with regard to homes worth around £250,000, where stamp duty jumps to 3%. It's much easier for an agent to shift a £249,000 house than a £250,500 one, because the stamp duty is so much less, £2,490 instead of £7,515. However, the difference in the agent's fee is minimal.

The Contract

Some common sense advice: before you sign the contract, read the small print and negotiate any contentious terms. You should make sure the time frame for the agreement is set out properly, and do not exceed three months, after which you are free to switch agents if you are dissatisfied. However, if you have a Sole Agency Agreement, I recommend that you push the term down a bit too approximately 6- 8 weeks, but no more. If you are not

sure what you are signing seek legal professional help. If you
sign the contract you are bound to the Terms and Conditions of
the Contract.

Contract Period

It is important to negotiate the shortest possible time period that
you are bound to your Estate Agent for selling your property.
The main reason here is that if you are unhappy with their
service you can terminate the contract very quickly and move to
another agent to sell your property. Some agents contracts may
vary and try to keep you tied to them for as long as six months.
A point to take note of here is that the longer your contract is
with an Estate Agent the less you are of a priority to them. Be
direct, tell the Estate Agent that you will only wish to instruct
them as your Sole Agent for a period of four weeks, after which
time you will either decide to keep them on or terminate the
contract upon five days written notice.

With short term contact you will find that the Estate Agent will
work a lot harder for you than long term contract as they want
the commission on the sale of your property not leave it to
another agent to get the commission on the sales of your
property. Any Estate Agent that objects to a four week contract
with a five-day notice period needs to be treated with caution,
this is because for example, if an agent is so confident in selling
your property, their valuation, their ability to find you the right
buyer now, and the level of service they provide. Then ask
yourselves why, would they need to take over four weeks to
prepare the sale of your property if they have a ready made
supply of client's line up to view your property.

Contract Period Ends

Like all forms of contract it is important to read the small print, as this is the part that there are clauses and sub-clauses that determine the stipulation of the contact you are signing. This is the Terms and Conditions that you are bound to in the eventually if things go wrong. For example, if you terminate Estate Agent X contract and later sells your property through another Estate Agent Z to a buyer that was originally introduced by your first Agent X. If you use an Estate Agent that is a member of the Ombudsman for Estate Agency (OEA) then at least they are bound to a Code of Practice that requires them to explain what happens in this situation.

The OEA's code allows for agents to make a claim for their commission if you sell to a buyer they originally introduced but could not convince the buyer to buy your property within six months of your contract ending. It is up to you to decide if six months is acceptable or not you can always get the clause changed. Be warned though, non-OEA Estate Agents can put what they like in their contracts. Some have even been know to contain clauses stating that no matter how much time passes, they will come after you for their fee if you sell to a buyer they originally introduced. Again, let me repeat my earlier advice: Read the contract carefully and think through the knock-on effects of each clause it contains. If you are unsure about anything there are four things you can do:-

- If you do not understand anything in the contract do not sign it.
- Cross out or change any clauses you find unacceptable.
- Send the contract to your conveyancing solicitor and ask for their advice on how to word any amendments you wish to make.
- Take your business elsewhere.

Contract Terms to Watch Out For

I would not recommend that you sign a contract that suggest the Estate Agent will be able to claim their fee if they find you a ready, willing and able purchaser of your property. This mean that if they found you a buyer and you, decide to pull out of the sale for any reason, you decide that the buyer is not suitable and choose not to sell to them, you will still have to pay the Estate Agents fees. How fair is that, say no to that straight away and have them draw up a new contract or have this amended so that you are not liable in any way.

Sole Selling Rights

With Sole Selling Rights this means that you grant the right for only one Estate Agent to market your property. For example, if you found a home buyer yourself and decided not to involve the Estate Agent, they would lawfully be within their rights to claim their fee. To be fair, you do not see many contracts using the term Sole Selling Rights these days but you should still watch out. However, you definitely need to be wary of Sole Agency Agreements that are worded in such a way as to effectively grant the agent Sole Selling Rights. To protect yourself against this it is wise to be familiar with the words that should be used in a Sole Agency Agreement.

The definition of Sole agency must be clearly written into the Estate Agent's "Terms and Conditions of Business and the standard wording should read:

Definition - Sole Agency

"You will be liable to pay remuneration to (Estate Agent's name), in addition to any other costs or charges agreed, if at any time unconditional contracts for the sale of the property are exchanged:

With a purchaser introduced by us during the period of our sole agency, or with whom we had negotiations about the property during that period, or
With a purchaser introduced by another agent during that period."

Point to note
Now, just so you know what to look out for, here's an example of how an Estate Agent has subtly altered the wording of a Sole Agency Contract to their advantage:

Definition - Sole Agency
"You will be liable to pay remuneration to (Estate Agent's name), in addition to any other costs or charges agreed, if at any time unconditional contracts for the sale of the property are exchanged:

With a purchaser introduced by us during the period of our sole agency, or with whom we had negotiations about the property during that period, or
With a purchaser introduced by another agent during that period, or

With a purchaser introduced by the vendor, other than those stated at the time of instruction or another agent during that period.

The additional line above is easy to miss, if you do not know what you are looking for.

However, it is the kind of thing that totally changes the nature of the agreement you are signing. I really feel that it is an underhand tactic. Insist on it to be removed from the contract and question the moral of the Agent and take your business elsewhere.

Estate Agents Fees

Check the contract and make sure you are clear on, who retains the authority to sign-off payment of the Estate Agent's fee. At what period is the Estate Agent becomes entitled to their fee. This will determine the type of contract you sign at the time when selling your property. Here are a few points to know that it is in your best interests to make sure that the fees are only payable on the completion of the Sale and not before. As some sales can still fall through between exchange and completion, therefore you want to make sure that fees are only paid on completion and not before. Some contracts will try to make you liable once exchange of contract has taken place. Once your Sale has been successful, the fees should become payable, and transferred to the agent, within a suggested time frame of at least five working days.

If for any reason your payment is late, what kind of penalty charges will the agent levy? Some agents make provision in their contracts to charge you unreasonable and hefty rates of interest. Make sure you check this charge and question it if you feel it is at an unfair or overly onerous level.

Some contracts are worded in such a way that once signed; you give away the right to withhold payment a perfectly reasonable thing for you to do if you wish to make a formal complaint about the Estate Agent's conduct during your sale. Be on the lookout for wording that gives your solicitor irrevocable instructions to pay the Estate Agents commission out of the sale proceeds. Have that clause taken out and replaced with something that leaves you in control over authorising the Estate Agent's Fee payment. It is best to have your conveyancing solicitor help you word this correctly.

ONLINE ESTATE AGENTS

An Online Estate Agents will provide you with a professional service and it is worth taking the time to understand exactly what they are, and what they do, they are not a private sale website. They operate in the same way as a traditional high street Estate Agent; they must fully comply with The Estate Agency Act 1979. Most online agent offer their service on a capped fee basis of around £500+VAT or on a 0.5 - 0.75%, no sale, no fee percentage basis. Most are members of the National Association of Estate Agents and The Estate Agency Ombudsman Scheme.

You have four options regarding the sale or purchase of your property. You can use the traditional high street Estate Agent, sell it yourself more on this later, sell it using via a Property Auction, more on this part later, or you can sell your Property Online through, an online agents. The arrival of the internet have made tradition Estate Agents to improve their property selling services and reduce their costs in order to be more competitive in the buying and selling process. Estate Agents that take this route, pass on the savings to the home seller are called Online Estate Agents.

One essential difference between an Online Estate Agency and that of a standard private sale website is unlike some of the 200 or so private sale websites out there, you cannot use an Online Estate Agency alongside a regular estate agent and hope to dodge their fee if you find your buyer online. For all intensive purposes, Online Estate Agents are estate agents. The rules are the same as if you appointed two high street estate agents to

simultaneously market your property. It would constitute a Joint
Sole Agency or Multiple Agency agreement and you would have
to pay both parties regardless of who finds your buyer.

Online estate agents usually have fewer offices than traditional
high street Estate Agents and offer coverage over a wider area.
Local knowledge may be lower than established local Estate
Agents whilst their internet presence and therefore their ability to
sell houses are generally greater. If you want to sell your
property quickly and economically but still want expert help then
I suggest that an Online Estate Agent could be the answer.
Online Estate Agent is growing at a fast rate, due to its
inexpensive and cost effective way of doing business that more
and more people are using these methods to buy and sell their
property. People are getting fed up with the high prices that they
have to pay the high street agents for their services that are not
cost effective.

With Online Estate Agents they offer a highly attractive
combination of high-reach online property advertising with low
fess options. As Online Estate Agents sales and purchases of
property becoming more and more common to that of tradition
High Street Estate Agents, means that most the buying and
selling can be done online without leaving your property. No
need to go to the high street Estate Agent on a cold windy day.
You can stay at home and market your property with the more or
less the same result that that of the High Street Agents. As more
of us now use the internet for virtually everything we want. Here
to the fact that buying and selling a property this way is a lot
easier than you think. First lower fees to pay the Agent compare
to that of the high street Agent. You are not limited to any one
Agent, your property can be seen by both locally and nationally,
wider area of coverage, options of different packages available
to choose from. With an Online Estate Agent it can be said to be
the new age internet marketing for property at a low cost. Here

you can save money with an online agent; they also offer a good service at low fees. Some online Estate Agents has a fixed-fee, some offer their market services for as little as £500, this increases, the details and option package that your require from the Online Estate Agents.

Online Estate Agent service is packed with superb features to assist you when selling a house. Most system is people friendly and easy to operate. Always make sure that before to sign up an Online Estate Agent that they are full members of the National Association of Estate Agents and the Ombudsman Scheme. By doing this, if some thing goes wrong you are protected and also have a complaints process that you can take up if you are not happy with the level of service that is provided. Some of the big names you will find are that of Rightmove, Findaproperty, Primelocation and Fish4homes, the list goes on, which offers fantastic and superb online marketing for your property. With Online Estate Agents your property can at any one time has the potentials of thousands in not more of potential buyers, because you are not limited to just locally for nationally, This can be said to be any one who is searching for a property in the region you are selling. Online Estate Agents will also advertise your property for sales on other property websites as well. Here you have more coverage for less money saving a lot of money compared to that of the high street Estate Agents.

When choosing an Online Estate Agent some of the things that you should know that are features with your list are that your property details are inserted into all of the UK's top Property search sites, this gives you more marketing power than traditional Estate Agents. You are provided with a dedicated website where your property details can be viewed by buyers. Property details are also placed on local newspaper websites, the company will manage all enquiries on your behalf, keeping organised is the hardest part of selling privately so it is important that you are provided with some help. They will arrange all viewings and call the buyer for feedback on you behalf. The Online Agent offers a service whereby they will negotiate all offers on your behalf, helpful if you do not wish to negotiate with buyers directly. Buyers are able to print sales particulars direct from your dedicated website. They provide a professional looking For Sale Board and install it at your property, Sale boards are shown to generate 30-50% of all enquires so this is essential for your sale to be successful. They will visit you at home to take an unlimited number of photos and measure your property for the production of floor plans (a handy service that needs to be done correctly and in accordance with the Property Misdescriptions Act 1991). A floor plan is produced for free. Floor plans are proven selling tools & something that few other private sale websites include.

 An Energy Performance Certificate can be arranged on your behalf. A virtual tour of your property is produced for free another proven selling tool. Your property is advertised until sold at no additional cost. If you choose an Online Estate Agent they will provides all of the above for you.

With an Online Estate Agency Services, you as a private property seller have the best chance of successfully selling your property and at the same time saving you thousands of pounds. This can be said to be cheapest, quickest and fastest way to get maximum coverage for a fraction of the price that of High Street Estate Agent. It has provided private individuals with access to the major property websites for example, Rightmove. Something that traditional private sale websites cannot do.

For a private seller, advertising with an Online Estate Agent is the best start you can make, however, to attract the maximum number of buyers you should consider advertising with an Online Estate Agent and one of the more popular Private Sale

Websites. There is very little crossover between where Online Estate Agent & Private Sale Websites advertise, so you do not need to worry about duplicate adverts overexposing your property. That will take the cost of selling your house up to around £500 - £650. When you consider that it costs 1.5-4% (UK average = £4,400) of your sale price to get the same internet exposure from an estate agent, you can see just what good value Online Estate Agent and Private House Sale Websites provide. Along with the pricing and presentation guidance you will find within this website, you have access to more than enough information to take control of your sale, sell for the best price and save many thousands of pounds.

PRIVATE HOUSE SALE

With Private House Sale, it simply means exactly that. You do all the work yourselves, from start to finish that is preparing your property for sale, organising the Energy Performance Certificate (EPC), taking pictures of your property and finally marketing your property. You are in total control as to how you want to market your property, using whatever means are available to use.

Here you will need maximum expose of your property in order for it to sell. A good starting point is to let every one knows that you are selling your property; this can be done via word of mouth, through family and friends. Have a For Sale Board outside the property with a contact telephone number. This way every one passing your property will see that you are selling your property, most important we have the use of the internet, here we can find websites that offers private selling, some of these are free to use as they will advertise your property for free, and some are paid advertising.

You could also place ads in local newspapers, as well as shops windows. Try to maximum your campaign exposure to sell your property as much as possible, using every means available to you to use. This is the cheapest method of all four ways to sell your property. These methods can be a hit or miss depending on where you are living. So think carefully before going along this route as to what time frame that you have in selling your property.

The success of any sales will depend on finding potential buyers for your property and where to look. There is always going to be buyers for properties. The questions here are; is the asking price of your property a true reflection on the property prices in your street and area? Is your property in a good state to be shown to potential buyers? If the answers to these two questions are yes then there will be a potential buyer.

Most buyers today are using the internet to find property to buy. They put in the search details of the type of property that they are interested in, for example, a three bedroom detached house in Bath, with a semi postcode to pin point the area that you most likely want to move to, lists upon lists of property in that area come will come up that are on sale, with pictures and details descriptions of the property. So by the time you go to the viewing of the property, the chances are that you are likely to know a great deal about the property already. All this is all done from the comfort of their own homes.

If you can grasp what I am trying to say here is that when you advertise your property on the internet use only good quality photographs, and a clear cut description of your property highlighting all the positive factors of your property. State the facilities and amenities within your property location, also good transportation links, and schools. These are all important elements that potential buyers are looking for.

When people are searching to buy property there are hundreds if not thousands of websites that have properties to buy or sell. Most people when searching for a property to buy normally just use the top five property sites on the internet. That is Rightmove, Fish4homes, Propertyfinder, Findaproperty and Primelocation. These five sites alone have over twelve million potential buyers and sellers and this is a conservative estimate. This is why it pays dividends to advertise on these sites because it is growing all the time. The biggest of these sites is Rightmove. Rightmove is responsible for every 2 out of 3 of all successful homeowners find their new homes. Over 97 percent of potential sales come from one of the top five sites. Simply if your property is not listed amongst these sites, then your property is not being marketed as effectively as it should and make take a long time to be sold as it is not been seen enough.

The success and willingness of the house buying public to embrace the internet has been a big problem for the newspaper industry, before, substantial revenue was made from Estate Agents advertising property for Sale. So, what has the newspaper industry done about this, simple, they bought the property sites. One must not forget that these sites you are looking at on the internet are largely own by Newspapers and Estate Agents, so whatever happens to the property market being advertise via the newspaper it makes no different to the newspaper because they gain revenue from which ever means you advertise. One of the main reasons why the internet has taken over the newspaper is that it is cheaper to upload your details onto the internet; it is there for a long period of time, updates can be done very quickly via your control panel where you are in control to make all the necessary amendments as you like. With regards to newspaper this can be very expensive due to print cost, out of date very quickly.

The reason for this is best illustrated by the actions of those companies that own the major property sites and guess what these are mostly own by newspapers apart form Rightmoves which is own by our good friend the Estate Agents (Halifax, Countrywide and Connells). Their actions explain why many private sellers fail and why you can have the utmost faith that you will be successful. Confused? Well, let me explain. When the property sites first started out you would be able to sign-up with a private sale website such as TheLittleHouse Company, HouseWeb, HouseLadder, Property Broker etc. and they would upload the details of your property onto the major websites.

With the current situation the following websites have all banned private sale websites including the new Tesco site, Rightmove, Primelocation, Propertyfinder, Findaproperty. I suspect this was due to pressure from or in order to please the Estate Agents who are their main clients and primary source of income and whose interest the websites must protect. The internet worked too well and the public were quickly realising, how easy it was to find buyers without the help of an agent, how little expertise it really took to sell property, how little it could cost to sell property. Finally there was proof that was no need to pay £1,000's to an estate agent, and soon everyone was going to know it. Doubtless this was very worrying for the UK's estate agents. The revolution had started and private sale websites had to be stopped. What does that tell you about the effectiveness of the private sale route?

In today world of the internet you can use any one of the 200 private sale websites to market your property will at best get you onto Fish4homes the weakest of the 5 major property and the only one to still allow private advertisers and a variety of secondary marketing platforms. They will put your property in front of about 3-4 million buyers per month. This is good but it is not as good as an Estate Agent who can reach an extra 9-10 million buyers per month with their access to Rightmove. Primelocation, Propertyfinder, Findaproperty. If you were planning on selling without an Estate Agent I would urge you not to use any of the 200 private sale websites as your only source of internet exposure, as you may well be under-marketing your property.

For a fraction of the cost of using a traditional Estate Agent, there are a limited number of services that give you access to all the major property websites and all of the important secondary sites that will put your property in front of about 30 million buyers and is significantly more than most Estate Agents can accomplish they usually advertise with only one or two of the major sites. It is certainly more than any private sale website can manage. These relatively new services are collectively called Online Estate Agents. If you want to cut out the middlemen and save a considerable sum of money then Online Estate Agents provide the means to do this successfully, value for money, a comprehensive and effective service, excellent customer service. Most of these websites ask you to fill out a simple form with the details of your property for sale, add some photos and your home for sale is listed, an important factor to mention is that if you are not in a chain, this can work in your favour, because there is no waiting, no contracts, no commissions, no fees, guaranteed and that is simple it.

Selling at a Property Auction

Property Auctions are a very effective way of selling a home very quickly. It is all over in a very short time frame from start to finish. That is you will have to hand over the keys 28 days after the auction date for your property. Make sure if this is your route of selling your property that you are properly organise as your time frame is very short 28 days. If you simply do not have the time or patience to find a home buyer from the traditional line of marketing your property, then a sale at a Property Auction may be your best solution. Selling at auction is best for people who want to sell their house as quickly as possible. Property Auction is becoming more common nowadays with the various property auction shows that can be seen now on television. So it is not as scary as when we first imagine it to be. Auction Houses are normally full with potential investors looking to purchase a property for a bargain price. Be realistic with your price and your property will be sold, be unrealistic and your property will be left behind as unsold.

Make sure you choose the right Property Auction House to sell your property that is one who is established and has a good reputation of a high level of investors attending. This involves picking an auctioneer who offers property similar to yours within the same price range. Choosing an unsuitable Property Auction greatly diminishes your chances of getting a favourable deal on your house. Also, obtain a property valuation before you decide on the reserve price in order to protect yourself against a highly unfavourable sale.

The Costs

The auctioneer will charge you for the advertisement in brochures and catalogues, a cost that you will have to cover regardless of whether your property is sold or not. You will also have to pay a commission of around 2.5 per cent of the sales price. Before signing any agreement, find out about all the expenses you will have to cover, even if your house is not sold.

Proceedings

Set the reserve price. This is based on your valuation; however, you should consult with the auctioneer before setting the price. Prepare a Contract, instructs your solicitor to prepare a contract which contains the Terms and Conditions of the Sale; this will be included in the auctioneer's brochure. Potential buyers will want to have a look at your house, and some will even want their surveyors to inspect it.

Completion

When the hammer falls, the sale is official and legally binding. The buyer will have to pay you 10 per cent of the agreed sales price straight away, the outstanding balance payable within 28 days after the auction. If he fails to do so, sue him or her.

Types of properties at auction

There are certain types of properties more suitable to be sold at auction than by normal means. These include:-

- Houses that are difficult to sell using an Estate Agent and are in a very bad state of repair and need substantial investment.
- Repossessed property usually needs to be sold as quickly as possible to cover the former owner's debts.
- Properties that are difficult to value and are unconventional in size and type.
- High demand properties that need little work or no work on and are in a prestigious location. The price paid for such properties can exceed their estimated market value substantially. .

The Disadvantages

You can never know how much your property will sell for. An auction is a highly volatile marketplace, if there is no demand on the day of your sale, you might end up selling it below its market value.

- You will have to pay your solicitor to be present at the auction in order to sort out any last-minute irregularities and answer questions. Depending on how enthusiastic your solicitor is about traveling, this can be quite a costly affair.
- Some people feel their privacy is violated at auctions, since the properties have to be open to potential buyers and their surveyors.
- Selling your house at auction can be more expensive than selling it via an Estate Agent. Also, you will have to cover certain expenses even if your property does not sell.

8. ENERGY PERFORMANCE CERTIFICATE

Making your property more energy efficient will provide buyers with reassurance that they will not be spending a vast sum of money on paying for energy consumption. Buyers are now using the Energy Performance Certificate as a method of lowering the asking price of property that does not have a high rating. By taking simple steps to insolate the loft area, tanks, filled cavity walls, and having double glazed windows will greatly improve the energy efficiency of your property. The government move toward Green Deals and new energy efficient methods we will see an increase in this area, with more wind farms and solo panel being used in our homes in the future.

The present Government has suspended HIP's as of 20th May 2010. Only the Energy Performance Certificate (EPC) are now required within 28 days of putting your property on to the market. You must also have commissioned an EPC before you market your property.

A number of changes are made to the Energy Performance of Building Regulations. In general the onus remains still with the Seller or Landlord to commission an EPC before marketing. The main changes are that the current 28 day period within which an EPC is to be secured using reasonable effects is reduced to 7 days. If after the 7 day period the EPC has not been secured the relevant person has a further 21 days to do so. New EPC Regulations should have come into force from 1st July 2011. This has now been delayed until further notice by the Department for Communities and Local Government (DCLG). This set back by DCLG mean that non-compliance of EPC will continue by Estate Agents and Landlords until this new regulation comes into force. A copy of the EPC should be attached to the marketing particulars of the property from October 2011

The main points are:-

- The EPC will be required within 7 days of commencement of marketing for property marketed after July 1st.
- Trading Standards Officers (TSO) are to be given more powers to request and enforce the EPC from Vendors, agents and landlords.
- The agents in both the residential and commercial market will now also be responsible for ensuring the EPC is available.
- The requirement to add the EPC to marketing material including the sales particulars, however, this has been delayed until October presumably to allow agents and portals to update their systems.

This means that Estate Agents will be required to produce evidence showing that an EPC has been commissioned where they are marketing a property. An important point here is that this new change is intended to remove the erroneous belief that the provision of an EPC can be delayed until shortly before the parties enter into a contract for Sale or Rent.

Recent Government changes that are to take place regarding Holiday Let Properties will be required in England and Wales to take effect from 30th June 2011. This means that an EPC will be required for a property rented out as a holiday let where the building is occupied as a result of a short term letting arrangement and is rented out for combined total of 4 months or more in any 12 month period.

All homes bought, sold or rented require an Energy Performance Certificate better known as an EPC for short. Below illustrates what a typical Energy Performance Certificates looks like. As you can see from this illustrate it is very similar to that you may have on your fridge already.

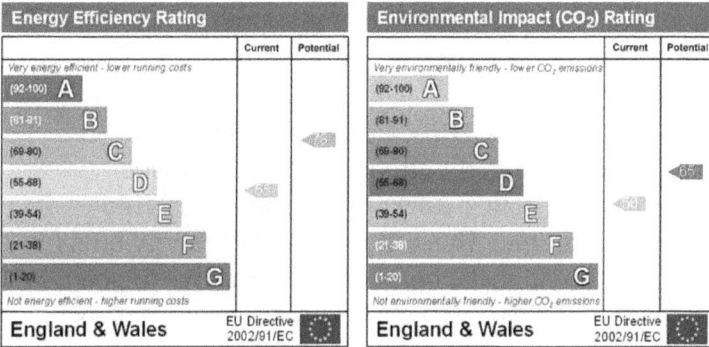

Energy Efficiency Rating			Environmental Impact (CO$_2$) Rating		
	Current	Potential		Current	Potential
Very energy efficient - lower running costs			Very environmentally friendly - lower CO$_2$ emissions		
(92-100) A			(92-100) A		
(81-91) B			(81-91) B		
(69-80) C			(66-80) C		
(55-68) D			(55-68) D		
(39-54) E			(39-54) E		
(21-38) F			(21-38) F		
(1-20) G			(1-20) G		
Not energy efficient - higher running costs			Not environmentally friendly - higher CO$_2$ emissions		
England & Wales	EU Directive 2002/91/EC		**England & Wales**	EU Directive 2002/91/EC	

Energy Performance Certificates tell you how energy efficient a home is on a scale of A-G. The most efficient homes - which should have the lowest fuel bills - are in band A.

The Certificate also tells you, on a scale of A-G; about the impact the home has on the environment. Better-rated homes should have less impact through carbon dioxide (CO2) emissions.
The average property in the UK is in bands D-E for both ratings. The Certificate includes recommendations on ways to improve the home's energy efficiency to save you money and help the environment.

Why is the Certificate important?

Nearly 40 per cent of the UK's energy consumption arises from the way in which our 25 million buildings are lit, heated and used. Even comparatively minor changes in energy performance and the way we use each building will have a significant effect in reducing energy consumption - and therefore carbon emissions. Communities and Local Government is leading the introduction of a number of energy and cost-saving measures to make all buildings more efficient. These measures are being applied across all European Union countries and are in line with the European Directive for the Energy Performance of Buildings.

The Energy Performance Certificate is part of these new measures to improve property efficiency. It will include suggestions to enable homeowners to improve the energy efficiency of the building. This can mean lower energy bills for the occupier, and could make homes more attractive to potential purchasers. The certificate will also provide contact details for the Energy Saving Trust who can help you find out whether you could be eligible for grants or discounts to help carry out these improvements to your home. It will also list simple ways that changes in behaviour can save you energy and money - without the need for any work.

How to Obtain an Energy Performance Certificate

If you are selling your Home or renting it out, it is your responsibility to provide an Energy Performance Certificate. The best place to look is in the Government Landmark Website. This will provide a list of Accredited Domestic Energy Assessor who can perform the EPC for you, other places to look are Google Search Engine, Telephone directories, websites etc. you will find a lot of Energy Assessor, want to do business with you. The Accredited Domestic Energy Assessor will under take the work of the Assessment of your property and produce Certificates. The alternative way is to sit back and let your Estate Agent do the work for you. This method is a bit more costly sometimes twice as much as if you were to find a Domestic Assessor yourself. Always ensure that the Domestic Assessor who is undertaking the work for you belongs to an Accreditation Scheme. By doing this you know that the work is carried out by a competent person with the correct skills that are needed to carry out the survey to a high standard set by the Accreditation.

If you are buying your home, whether it is old or new there is no need to obtain an Energy Performance Certificate, as the seller of the property will provide one, free of charge. If no Energy Performance Certificate is provided, your solicitor will need to contact the seller as to why none is provided. If you are not given an Energy Performance Certificate that you are entitled to you can contact Trading Standards of your Local Authority as Trading Standards have the power to issue a fixed penalty notice of £200 for domestic property that do not have an EPC. If it is a newly built property you should contact your Building Control Department of your Local Authority. The Sale of the property cannot be completed unless an EPC is completed, as it is a legal requirement when a building is built, sold or rented.

An Energy Performance Certificates is Valid for 10 Years. The cost of an EPC will depend of the size of your property and also, on the current market forces. An EPC will cost more if you let your Estate Agent do this work for you. Some times twice as much as if you do it for yourselves.

If you are not happy with your EPC Report, because, for example, your property has double-glazed windows and the assessor say that you have single glazed windows. This will results in giving your property the wrong rating. The first thing is to contact the Domestic Energy Assessor who carried out the Report and state your reason why this Report is wrong. If he/she refuses to change it make an official complaint in writing following the complaints process the Domestic Energy Assessor has in place. If the complaint has not been resolved to your satisfaction, you can take this up with the Domestic Energy Assessor Accreditation Scheme. That is the reasons why it is essential to have someone who is carrying out the survey of your property that belongs in an Accreditation Scheme.

WORK OF A DOMESTIC ENERGY ASSESSOR

When the Domestic Energy Assessor arrives, he (or she) will need to inspect, and make note of, the following property details:

The visual inspection, which should normally take less than an hour will involve: -

- Measurements of interior / exterior of property.
- Walls and roof construction.
- Signs of wall cavity fill insulation.
- Number of open or closed fireplaces.
- Make and model of boiler and type of flue and fuel used.
- Inspection of energy savings devices.
- Type of heating systems used and controls.
- Measure roof insulation.
- Measure the thickness of any hot water jackets or foam insulation.
- Check for excessive window are in larger houses and take measurements of conservatories and Extensions.
- Note the number of habitable rooms that are heated.
- Sketch and make notes relating to property room layout.
- Take photographs of the above for evidence

Which building needs an EPC?

To keep it simple in contact, an EPC is required when a building is either sold or rented and is of a construction that the property has wall, roof, and uses Energy to heat the interior of the property. The construction of the building can be a whole building or part of a building that has it own facilities for example, own heating system, own front entrance, bathroom. Not shared with any other adjacent property. Hope you get the picture. If you are not sure whether your property needs an EPC or not, go to the Government website, or contact your Estate Agent or an Accredited Domestic Energy Assessor.

Which buildings do not need an EPC?

Again to keep this part simple. We can say that an EPC is not required when a building is built, rented or sold, if it is a place of worship, industrial sites, workshops and non-residential agricultural buildings that do not use a lot of energy, standalone buildings with total useful floor area of less than 50 square metres that are not used to provide living accommodation for a single household, temporary buildings that will be used for less than two years.

"Please note that an Energy Performance Certificate is valid for 10 Years from the date of issue"

9. SOLICTOR AND CONVEYANCING

Finding the right solicitor or conveyancer can mark the difference between a smooth and a stressful move to your new property. A property Specialist Solicitor can make a world of difference and also the process can be completed very quickly. Most of us already have a solicitor or know of one. If you do not have a solicitor, one of the best means of finding a suitable solicitor or conveyancer is through personal recommendation, so ask friends and family who have bought a property in the area or the Estate Agent or mortgage broker. I recommend that you compare at least 3 solicitors in the areas. This takes away the process of one being recommended by the mortgage company. This applies to both buyer and seller. Here are some guidelines to help you make the right choice. Do not be afraid to ask as many questions as you like when choosing a solicitor because at the end of the day it is you who will be paying for the service provided.

What a solicitor's role is.

It can be said to be the process of buying and selling a property. Conveyancing is the part of legal process to transfer the ownership of a property from the seller to the buyer. The vast majority of people usually opt to hire a solicitor or licensed conveyancer for their conveyancing purposes. All solicitors practising law in England and Wales must also be registered with the Law Society. There are separate societies for Northern Ireland and Scotland when you are buying a property; your solicitor generally works on behalf of your mortgage lender, who has a vested interest, as they are the one who is going to lend you the Loan or Mortgage. The Mortgage Lender usually insists on a number of certain searches before they will release the money for your house.

Whereas the sellers, solicitor of conveyancer will draw up a contract for the sale. The Sellers will also need to produce an Energy Performance Certificate (EPC). The solicitor will also apply for the title deeds from your mortgage lender. They will also organise searches for example, the EPC, and send a list of questions to the buyer's solicitor.

As soon as you make an offer on a property, your Estate Agent or individual seller will ask for your solicitor's details to pass onto the seller's solicitor. It is therefore important to have a solicitor ready when you start look for a property to avoid having to make important decision in a hurry or rush. This way you can pay full attention to the property that you are going to purchase. A solicitor's job is to take care of all legal aspects of moving house. Here are some things you should consider when choosing a conveyancer, whether you are buying or selling a property. Your solicitor will conduct a range of tasks on your behalf, whether you're buying or selling a property, or both. The general tasks include:-

- Local Authority Search.
- Title and Land Registry Search
- Stamp duty.
- Drainage & Water Search.
- Energy Performance Certificate.
- Chancel Search if in a Parish Area.
- Coal Mining and Environmental Search.
- Managing the collection and transfer of funds.
- Providing legal advice and recommendations.
- Drawing up and assessing contracts.

Apart from the conveyancing work there is also the lender's legal work to be done. Your conveyancer could act for the lender, which should save you money. The principal task is to draw up a mortgage deed, which sets out the conditions of your loan. The lender will hold this and the title deeds of your property until the loan is paid in full.

Cost

Solicitors charge their clients in a variety of ways. Some solicitors may charge a fixed fee, while others will charge you a percentage based on the value of the house or flat in question. In addition, there may be extra fees to cover the cost of paperwork, any complex issues that require additional work, or if the process requires more time and attention than anticipated. It is a good idea to obtain at least three quotes from different companies. Make sure that you know what costs the quote includes. You will usually be charged for the conveyancer's time, phone calls, letters and faxes and their indemnity fee. They may state that if any unforeseen problems arise these will be dealt with through an extra charge.

Costs can range from between £600 to £1,500, depending on the work involved and the value of the property in fees. However, the cost will also depend on whether your property is leasehold or freehold. Leasehold properties will cost more as they involve additional work checking the lease. Most conveyancers will ask for payment of land registry and local authority search fees in advance. A solicitor will also charge for any additional costs they incur dealing with your transaction, such as postage costs, VAT, etc. These are known as disbursements. The balance will be due on completion.

Some people choose to cut out the property solicitor or conveyancer and manage the conveyancing process themselves in order to save money. This is a high-risk strategy and it is sensible to use the professionals and instruct a qualified property solicitor. Do not be tempted to opt for professionals that are offering a cheap deal, this could mean that they are dealing with many clients, which will more often result in a slow service. As this is probably the highest investment that you will make, it is important to get right first time.

Once you have chosen a conveyancer they will ask to see some form of identification, such as a passport or driving licence, and your mortgage lender's details.

The key process for both buyers and sellers in England and Wales are as below. Scotland has a separate system. A more in-depth coverage of buying and selling will be covered in the Buying and Selling Chapters of this book. What I want to do here is to highlight the process only so that you are aware of the stages that are involved in Buying and selling a property.

Buying a property in England & Wales:-

- Stage 1 - Agreement of sale
- Stage 2 - Exchange of contracts
- Stage 3 – Completion

Buying a property in Scotland:-

- Stage 1 - Before an offer
- Stage 2 - Making an offer
- Stage 3 - Concluding an offer

Selling a property in England & Wales:-

- Stage 1 - Agreement of sale
- Stage 2 - Exchange of contracts
- Stage 3 - Completion

Selling a property in Scotland:-

- Stage 1 - Before an offer
- Stage 2 - Making an offer

- Stage 3 - Concluding an offer

Once you have found a property to buy, you will most likely need to instruct a chartered surveyor who will check the structural condition of the building on your behalf. The mortgage provider will conduct its own valuation of the property, but most people want the reassurance of their own dedicated structural survey on the property they wish to buy. Before you choose a surveyor, make sure you know which kind of survey you need and what you're expecting the surveyor to produce. This is likely to depend on what kind of home you are planning on purchasing.

Type of Survey

The type of property you are buying should be the based as to what type of survey you should choose to provide you with the information you need. For example, do I need a Homebuyer's Report; is a mortgage survey adequate enough or do I need a Full Building Survey? This can be determined by the age of the property, if it is a listed building, the style, the design and even problems you may have witnessed while at the viewing on your behalf.

Knowledge of the Local Area

The surveyor should have a good knowledge of the local area and has a various degree of knowledge of houses and flats within its locality as to the age of the property type of brick or stone that is used in the area. If you are buying a very particular type of property, such as a listed building or a very unusual construction type, having specialists and experience in such properties can make the process a lot easier to survey as they will be looking for any unusual problems that are known in the area. It can save a lot of time if you use a local solicitor with a sound knowledge of local laws and leasehold. However, if you are keen for the process to move as quickly as possible, you might want to consider hiring a firm that is within close proximity to where you live or work. If you can visit them in person, you can save a lot of time by avoiding documents going to and from the post.

Costs Consideration

The cost of a survey should always be a consideration when choosing a surveyor. You should contact at least three surveyors for a cost comparison. The cost of a survey varies a great deal. Avoid just choosing the cheapest ones, as this may indicate a poorer service. If you know of someone who has just recently purchase their property, ask if they did a good job and the cost of the survey. Again recommendation can be the best way to find a suitable Surveyor. A guide table below indicates what you should expect to pay for a survey, this will vary by survey that you have requested from the surveyor, and also by the value of the property, its size and by which region of the country you live in.

What can you expect from the surveyor?

One of the most important things when dealing with your surveyor is to ask as many questions that you have, even if it seems silly to you. By asking as many questions that you have it will give you an indication as to what to expect from the surveyor for example, can they work to your deadline, how long will they take to complete the Survey Report, the work that they are about to undertake. It is going to be your property, therefore seeks clarification on exactly what the work will be, what involvement and detail will the survey ascertain, this way you will not be disappointed if certain work is not done or expected to be inspected in the property. The surveyor should inform you of what you should expect from the property, depending on which survey you chose to have done on the property.

Choosing a surveyor

Try and avoid a conveyancing solicitor who is over-worked, or who may be too junior. You want their full attention and experience to make sure no important details are missed. You should try and source a solicitor that you trust and feel that you can work well with. Make sure that the solicitor takes the time to explain everything to you in detail. If there is anything you don't understand, make sure everything is explained in layman's terms. Again ask as many questions as possible until you are happy with the answers that you are given and that you can understand.

Once you have worked out which type of survey to go for, the next task is to find a suitable surveyor. One of the best way to find and choose a surveyor is by recommendation from your friends, family, Mortgage Broker or your Estate Agent, for further help you can contact the Royal Institution of Chattered Surveyors which represents around 80,000 qualified surveyors, if all other options fail to find someone suitable.

Online conveyancing

Once you get your conveyancing quote you can then instruct the conveyancer to proceed and have a solicitor take up your case instantly. You will be provided with all the information you need to contact your solicitor and pass the details on to your property agent or mortgage company. Some property solicitors offer the opportunity for clients to track the progress of their property transaction online. This means that you can access your particular case online 24 hours a day to see how it is progressing. In some cases, you can also receive updates via e-mail and text message and all the documentation dealt with through the post, cutting out visits to the solicitor's offices. Throughout the process you can monitor the progress of your case via the conveyancing solicitor's website and post questions or queries instantly for your solicitor to act on. You deal with a solicitor directly in the same way you would do if they were a local solicitor.

Property Surveys

It is estimated that only about 20% of all homebuyers commission a professional survey when buying their property. I strongly recommend that you have a full survey done, when visiting a property that you are about to purchase, the first time you may only have a quick viewing of the property and you can not see the full scale of the property as it may be in the night time, or you may be distracted. You must remember that with a short time frame you can not see every thing like that of a professional Surveyor for example, the full structure of the building as to damp, leaking gutters, the satiability of the property. This is somewhat surprising considering that buying a property is probably the biggest purchase investment in most people's lives. One explanation for this low take up is that many homebuyers believe the mortgage lender's survey is sufficient.

The Mortgage lender's survey is simply a mortgage valuation on the property, all this is a property inspector visit the property and condition of the property to establish the level and terms of the mortgage loan. This survey will not tell you if the property is worth the price you are paying for it, or point out any structural defects in the property. You will need to have a chartered surveyor inspection of the property for a more structured fault finding survey, which can save a lot of money and time in the future, as you will know the true state of the property that you are purchasing. Before you sign any contracts make sure that you know the state of the property that you are going to purchase so that there is no surprise waiting for you in the near future. There are two main types of survey when purchasing a property that you need to know: - The Homebuyer's Report and the Building Survey.

Homebuyer's report

The Homebuyer's Report Survey is designed to keep costs to a minimum and is more likely to be the best choice if the property you are buying is conventional in type, built and construction that is in a modern property style in good and in a reasonable condition that has been built within the last 20-30 years. The survey will focus on the defects and problems that are urgent and likely to have an effect on value of the property. The Royal Institution of Chartered Surveyors, (RICS) state that the main objectives of the Homebuyer's Report are to:

- Make a reasoned and informed judgement on whether or not to proceed with the purchase.
- Assess whether or not the property is a reasonable purchase at the agreed price.
- Make clear what decisions and actions should be taken before contracts are exchanged.

Building survey

The Building Survey is suitable for all residential properties and provides a more in-depth scale or picture of the property's construction and condition. A greater level of details is in the Building survey compared to that of the Homebuyer's Report. This type of survey is required when a property is of an unusual construction or has had extensive alterations, if it is an old building, listed building, in need of serious structural repair or if you are planning a major conversion or renovation.

The Building Survey Report will include detailed technical information on the construction of the property, materials used in construction of the property, a listing of all major and minor defects in the property. The cost of a Building Survey is more expensive than a Homebuyer's Report because of the time and more details the survey is. You can expect the final report within three working weeks of the original survey. The average cost of a Building Survey normally start from £480 upwards and will usually take one to two days to complete.

10. DIFFERENT PROPERTIES TYPES

All you need to know about Buying and Selling your Property

All you need to know about Buying and Selling your Property

All you need to know about Buying and Selling your Property

11. USFUL CONTACT LISTS

The National Association of Estate Agents
Arbon House
6 Tournament Court
Edgehill Drive
Warwick
CV34 6LG
Tel - 01926 496800

The Leasehold Advisory Service (LEASE)
Maple House
149 Tottenham Court Road
London W1T 7BN
Tel: 020 7383 9800
Fax: 020 7383 9849
Website: www.lease-advice.org.uk

The Council for Licensed Conveyancers
16 Glebe Road
Chelmsford
Essex CM1 1QG
Tel: 01245 349599
Website: www.conveyancer.org.uk

Financial Ombudsman Service
South Quay Plaza
183 Marsh Wall
London
E14 9SR
Tel: 0845 080 1800
Website: www.financial-ombudsman.org.uk

All you need to know about Buying and Selling your Property

The Law Society
113 Chancery Lane
London
WC2A 1PL
Tel: 020 7242 1222
Website: **www.lawsociety.org.uk**

National House Building Council (NHBC)
Building House
Chilern Avenue
Amersham
Buckinghamshire
HP6 5AP
Tel: 01494 735363

Energy Performance Certificate
HIP Home Direct
133 West Bromwich Road
Walsall
West Midlands
WS1 3HP
Tel: 01922 633 692
Websites: **www.hiphomedirect.co.uk**

Inland Revenue
www.inlandrevenue.gov.uk

12. INDEX

www.ingramcontent.com/pod-product-compliance
Lightning Source LLC
Chambersburg PA
CBHW051958090426
42741CB00008B/1451